FIGHTING BACK

FIGHTING BACK

One Man's Struggle for Justice against the British Army

Barry Donnan

MAINSTREAM
PUBLISHING
EDINBURGH AND LONDON

To M.S. Power – without your help and generous advice,
this book would not have been possible.

Copyright © Barry Donnan, 1999
All rights reserved
The moral right of the author has been asserted

First published in Great Britain in 1999 by
MAINSTREAM PUBLISHING COMPANY (EDINBURGH) LTD
7 Albany Street
Edinburgh EH1 3UG

ISBN 1 84018 171 0

A catalogue record for this book is available from the British Library

Typeset in Caslon
Printed and bound in Great Britain by Butler & Tanner Ltd

Contents

1. In the Beginning   7

2. Murder in the Sky   16

3. Cambridge   28

4. It's a Jungle Out There   46

5. You Could Knock Me Down with a Feather   82

6. On the Run   110

7. Marking Time   135

8. Ireland   155

9. Down but Not Out   162

10. Legalities   175

It is not the critic who counts nor the man who points out how the strong man stumbles or where the doer of deeds could have done better. The credit belongs to the man who is actually in the arena, whose face is marred by dust and sweat and blood, who knows great enthusiasm, great devotion and the triumph of achievement, and who, at worst, if he fails at least he fails whilst daring greatly, so that his place shall never be with those cold and timid souls who know neither victory nor defeat. You've never lived until you've almost died. For those who have had to fight for it, life truly has a flavour the protected shall never know.

Theodore Roosevelt

1. In the Beginning

The effect of the ice-cold water was indescribable. Our training corporal had ordered us to stand underneath a fast-flowing waterfall. It was early November and bitterly cold. This was our instructor's method of making sure we had waterproofed our kit adequately.

'Move your arses and jump into the river!' the corporal screamed at us.

Once across the river we struggled out of the water and on to the bank, then we had to complete a ten-mile speed march over Otterburn training-range.

This was 'Exercise First Strike', which is a basic introduction to army field manoeuvres. I was now Fusilier Donnan, a recruit of the Junior Infantry Battalion at Ouston, Newcastle. My platoon was a mixture of Scottish and English with the average age being 16. The training was very gruelling and a shock to the system, it was a very physical existence. The first five weeks were a blur of bullshit, running and more bullshit. (Bullshit is an army term which is applied to boring and stupid tasks and also covers all the shouting, cleaning and times of being fucked around.) I found out that I was good at running and loved the time spent in the gym. I actually started to enjoy it.

My instructor was a typical Glasgow hard man and was one of the old school who enjoyed slapping and inflicting mental pain on the weaker recruits. During morning inspection he would have the whole room standing at attention for an hour. Then he would scream: 'Stand by your bed!' and he would swagger into the room, not bothering to inspect any kit.

Then he would yell: 'Torpedo positions, go.'

This was our cue to change places with the recruit standing directly opposite. The instructor would then whistle a tune while we trashed each other's lockers and beds. The room would be like a bombsite, kit strewn everywhere. 'Two minutes to get the kit away and then get outside.'

Once outside, my section would march at the double all over the camp until we were exhausted. It was hard work, but I started to feel and act like a soldier.

Weekends would come and we would lie in bed all day Saturday, trying to catch up on much-needed sleep. We couldn't even drink as we were all underage.

The training became more and more intense. We'd be out in the field one or two nights during the week, learning how to dig a trench and defend attacks from the enemy.

Back in camp we had to wash all our kit, dry it and then press it for the next locker inspection in the morning. It had to be immaculate, but no matter how hard we tried it was never good enough. Hour after hour was spent on the drill-square practising for our passing-out parade. I hated every minute of drill; I always ended up in the guardroom and got a good beasting (a very hard training session) from the provost sergeant, who was the biggest bastard in the world. We would be doubled around the exercise-yard holding a fire extinguisher above our heads. It was so painful that nearly everyone came back in tears.

One morning I was marching to the cookhouse for breakfast when the provost sergeant walked past me. I put my head down and carried on. 'Get back here, you wanker!' he shouted. I turned round and realised he was shouting at me, so I ran over and halted. 'Do you fancy me, you fucking tart?'

'No, Sergeant,' I said, panicking.

'Well, don't fucking smile at me then.'

I had never smiled at this madman, but I wasn't going to argue in case he killed me or beat me up.

'Report to the guardroom tonight showing smile removed from face – now fuck off!'

'Yes, Sergeant.'

That night I dressed in full uniform and marched to the guardroom, wondering how to show my smile was removed from my face. He inspected my uniform, then inside my ears and finally the soles of my boots. Then he asked where the smile was. I was speechless. So, because I couldn't show him the smile, he told me to report again the following night. I asked my instructor's advice and was told to 'use a pen and draw it on your hand'.

It worked and the provost sergeant even smiled.

Weapon training was great and I really enjoyed it. During one lesson I was messing around with the rifle and put an empty magazine in it and cocked the weapon. Unknown to me, the instructor had been watching. He called me over, unloaded the rifle, then hit me on the head with it. After that I never messed around with weapons again.

After three months we had our first leave. Back home I met up with a few old mates, but things had changed. Even after such a short time in the army my views were completely different. I had been brainwashed and was a very different person. After a week at home I was desperate to get back to the army and my new mates.

Back at the depot we trained relentlessly for another eight weeks. The final couple of weeks were spent on the drill-square and preparing our best uniforms for the big day of our passing-out parade.

My parents came down to watch the passing-out parade and I felt really proud marching to the sound of the bagpipes and performing my rifle drill in front of my family. My mother and father met all my instructors and were given a guided tour of the camp, then we had lunch. I had completely fallen in love with being a soldier. I knew I had made the right choice about joining the army; I wanted to be a soldier forever.

After a couple of weeks' leave I reported to Milton Bridge – just outside Edinburgh – as we still had to complete eight weeks' adult training before we could be posted to our respective regiments. The English contingent on the course was posted to a training depot in Yorkshire and we had a new training team, that was about the only difference. As a group we were treated more like adults and given a bit more responsibility and freedom. My instructor was a member of the Argyll and Sutherland Highlanders. He was a hard man and we all tried to keep on his good side.

We spent a lot of time on the ranges with various weapons, as our handling drills had to be perfect. Corporal Headbutt, as we named him, for obvious reasons, had an imaginary gym on a patch of grass, if you made a mistake on the range, then that is where you went. He had a prearranged routine of exercises and stress positions; depending on how badly you fucked up would determine your length of stay. It was a killer. During a defence exercise on the Pentland Hills we had to dig four-man fire trenches, which give you protection from air and ground attacks, and this can take nearly two days. We had worked all through the night in the pouring rain, we were caked in mud and still only halfway down. Morale was at an all-time low when Corporal Headbutt came to see us just after first light.

'Get out of my fucking way, I'll show you how it's done,' he boomed, grabbing the pickaxe from me. He then started swinging the pickaxe like a madman. We huddled in a small group and looked on, shivering in the cold.

'You lot better fucking switch on,' he was muttering.

He swung the axe so far he hit himself right on top of the

head. He rolled backwards and wriggled in pain. I have never wanted to laugh so much in my life. Morale was lifted immediately and we carried on digging while we had a laugh in the bottom of the trench.

Our time at Milton Bridge passed quickly. Most weekends were free and we could travel home; everyone was now eager to get to their respective regiments. We all felt like big, grown-up and hard soldiers. We had a final passing-out parade, which was a big affair and all my friends and family turned up. It pissed with rain all day, but after nine months of training I was glad my training was all over. We handed in our kit and said goodbye to mates that we might never see again.

After ten days' leave I reported to 1 RHF (Royal Highland Fusiliers) at Redford Barracks, Edinburgh. I felt excited and yet quite nervous as I'd heard lots of nasty stories about older guys giving the new guys a really hard time. Initiation rituals were commonplace in the army at that time. Apparently, in the RHF they pulled your trousers down and exposed your bare arse, then sunk their teeth in your cheeks till you screamed. As far as I was concerned these were all rumours and something I would deal with when it happened. I was given a welcome by the commanding officer (CO), who at that time was Lt-Col D.H. Hills. I was then posted to 5 Platoon, Bravo Company.

My new platoon sergeant had recently been promoted and was very switched on. I was given a room of my own and my arrival went more or less unnoticed. Compared to the training depot, the discipline was fairly relaxed. After we had finished our work for the day, we could book out and then head into the city.

My rifle platoon consisted of 20 soldiers and our first couple of weeks were spent bumming around doing very little. The regiment had ceremonial commitments at Edinburgh Castle, so everyone else seemed too busy to worry about what I was doing.

One morning the sergeant-major ordered: 'Donnan, outside

and count all the windows in the barracks.' This was army mentality, giving out fruitless tasks for the sake of it.

At weekend the camp was a riot. You had blokes who'd been privates for ten or 12 years going out on the piss, then coming in and smashing up the place. I slept with the door locked and my bedside cabinet pushed against the door, just in case.

It was now early December 1988 and the regiment was starting to prepare for a four-year posting in Cambridge. Most of the old sweats were not happy about being posted to England; they all seemed so negative, everything was a hassle. After my training I was still full of enthusiasm and I wanted to create a good impression so I kept my mouth shut. The next two weeks were spent scrubbing the barracks and packing our kit ready for the move to Oakington Barracks, near Cambridge. The whole regiment was looking forward to Christmas leave as this would be the first complete Christmas leave without any commitments for almost ten years. The fact that we were based in Scotland made it even more special. At 17 I was the youngest in the regiment and it was customary that I would toast the commanding officer at the Christmas dinner. I was quite nervous, in fact I was terrified, about standing up and speaking in front of the regiment.

Ten days before leave was due to start we had a FIBUA (fighting in a built-up area) exercise to complete at Dalbeattie. The GOC (General Officer Commanding) of Scotland had been invited as a guest, so everything had to be very slick. On the morning of the exercise we boarded our four-tonne trucks and headed for Dalbeattie. I was eager to get stuck in and show the company what I was made of. After a couple of hours we arrived, absolutely freezing, to be told to 'hurry up and wait'. The assault would not start for another two hours, the GOC was running late. Meanwhile, the platoon sergeant gave us a lecture on his favourite subject: how to kill things. When the GOC arrived, we headed out to the start line for the attack. My section had to cross a broad river to reach the LUP (lying-up point) where the advance would start; everything was on strict timings. On reaching the riverbank we all came to a halt while we searched for a shallow area so we could cross over. I was over-keen to impress and stepped into what I thought was knee-deep water. I disappeared beneath the surface for a few seconds. On surfacing again, all I heard was laughter and shouts: 'Who's a silly cunt then?' I was drenched and felt really stupid, but I was still determined to put a good attack in. On the given word of command we advanced towards the old buildings, my weapon placed against my shoulder so that I was ready to fire. As we got outside the door I slipped the safety catch off, the section commander then kicked in the door and we all went for it. Systematically we cleared the building, room by room, everyone seemed confused about what was going on. Lots of blank rounds were being fired, everyone was shouting and screaming. We moved through the building in what seemed like no time, it had all happened so quickly. Outside, I was knackered. We unloaded our weapons and had a debrief. The attack had taken just over an hour. I couldn't believe time had passed so quickly.

'Who are you?' the GOC asked.

'Fusilier Donnan, sir.'

Then he asked a set of questions that every senior officer asks, it must be something they learn at Sandhurst: 'Enjoying yourself? Food all right? What do you enjoy most about the army?'

'You look very sweaty,' he said.

'No, sir, I fell in the river, sir,' I replied.

I couldn't believe he thought I looked sweaty, no one can be that stupid, then I wondered if he was taking the piss. The platoon sergeant told me in no uncertain manner that all officers were mentally retarded pondlife. I was learning fast how life in the army really is.

Back in the barracks we started packing kit and placing it in boxes ready for the move down to England. Next morning the whole regiment took part in the CO's cross-country run, which was more for fun than anything else. The regiment was on a high, everyone was so excited about going on leave and Christmas was only four days away. Later that night, my platoon had a piss-up in a local bar just outside the camp. We were all slowly getting drunk and having a good laugh while, unknown to us, a major catastrophe was unfolding less than a hundred miles away. A nightmare had come true. As time passed, the bullshit started flowing – along with the booze – and we sat listening to the platoon sergeant, who was describing how to eat toads in the jungle. Anyway, at some point, the duty officer appeared, dressed in full combat, which was most unusual. 'Everyone back to camp now,' ordered the colour sergeant. Some of the senior blokes were moaning because they had just bought a round of drinks. The colour sergeant was not in the mood for any hassle. 'Get your fucking arses back to camp right now, or you're going in the jail,' he said, looking well pissed off.

We all grabbed our jackets and ran the two miles back to the barracks. Once inside the camp it was obvious that something was going on; there were trucks being moved on to the parade square and the place was chaotic. We were ordered to unpack our kit and get changed into full combats, we then sat around the main corridor waiting for some news as we knew nothing. Rumour control started spreading a couple of stories, but nothing had been confirmed. Some people took great delight in making up imaginative stories and it was amazing how quickly they spread around the regiment. After about 40 minutes the platoon commander arrived to give us a briefing. He told us that an RAF jet had crashed on to a petrol station somewhere in the Borders.

'Any questions?' asked the boss.

'Does this mean leave is cancelled, sir?'

'I have no idea what is happening. Get some sleep until we get further orders.'

I lay down and tried to sleep on my kit bag but my head was spinning. I felt a hangover starting to take effect. I didn't care about anything other than going on leave. We all sat and waited. It was a typical scenario – you are told to hurry up and wait and that everything must be done in double-quick time, then you end up sitting around for hours. Army mentality means it looks better if you do it faster, with lots of shouting, even though you may end up sitting around doing fuck all for ages. None of it makes sense.

I remember waking up cold and confused; I had been sleeping for only 30 minutes. I remember hearing the boss telling us to bring sleeping bags, then to head to the square. Thoughts of Christmas leave rapidly vanished. The whole of B Company was formed up and a roll-check was called by the sergeant-major.

'Listen in everyone, a jumbo jet has crashed in the Borders. We've been called in to assist, that's all I know at the moment,' said the company commander. 'Get on the transport and let's go.'

All I can remember thinking is: 'Where the fuck did he come from?' I had been in the regiment almost six weeks and I had never seen him before. We climbed on the trucks and crawled into our sleeping bags. No one spoke a word, we all had the same thoughts: Christmas was only four days away, leave was more important than any crashed aircraft – or so we thought. It was a freezing cold night and very quickly we were on the dark back roads heading south.

2. Murder in the Sky

I awoke two hours later in agony. It felt as if someone was standing on my head. I opened my eyes and realised that Les was, in fact, standing on my head in an attempt to look out of the truck. The sky was glowing red and, even though we still had five or six miles to travel, we could clearly see several huge fires burning away. I tried to think of a jumbo jet and the mess it would make. I couldn't imagine it.

As we drove into the small town of Lockerbie, it looked like hell. Blue flashing lights and fires lit up the town, while every street was blocked with police cars and fire engines, all of which were trying to get through. Rubble and mud had showered the town like rain, nowhere was untouched. It was now 0200 hours – less than eight hours since the disaster had happened – and we were the first army unit to be deployed to Lockerbie. Realisation of what we were involved in hit me like a stone.

'No fucking Christmas leave for us fuckers,' someone shouted. We all laughed, but it was a forced, nervous laugh.

The trucks stopped and we were taken inside Lockerbie Primary School, which had been set up as incident head-quarters. Once inside we grabbed seats in the canteen, which was a hive of activity with the Salvation Army working non-stop to provide tea and hot food to police and fire crews who had worked through the night. We sat in small groups and discussed our future role over the next couple of days. No one could tell us anything at this stage. One thing, however, was certain: the chances of finding survivors were rapidly diminishing. During the night more help arrived in the form of mountain-rescue teams, an RAF regiment and several more helicopters. The platoon sergeant told us to get some sleep and most of us crashed out on the tables.

Within 40 minutes I could feel someone shaking me, it was John, the company storeman. 'Wake up, wake up,' he was saying. 'The TV cameras will be coming round in five minutes, the major wants everyone sitting up.' Shortly afterwards the major came in and ordered us to sit up straight. The major's comments brought a few baffled looks from the surrounding soldiers.

One bloke said: 'The cunt will have us standing at attention in full number twos next [a dress uniform used only on special occasions].'

I tried not to laugh, but I could see this kind of bullshit didn't wash with some of the senior blokes very well. The cameras eventually appeared an hour later, again it was a case of 'hurry up and wait'.

At first light some of the helicopter crews started coming in for tea breaks; we quizzed them for details. Most of them looked pale and upset. They told us that the wreckage was spread over 100 square miles and that no one could possibly have survived such a crash.

At 0600 hours I had some breakfast and a wash as I knew it would be a hard day at the office for us. The platoon sergeant came into the canteen and ordered us all outside for a briefing in the car park. We were given a very short briefing on the areas that we had been asked to search and the boss also warned us that under no circumstances were we to touch any wreckage of the aircraft. Before we climbed on the trucks someone asked: 'What can we expect to find, sir?'

'Get on the truck, you idiot,' answered the boss.

Here we were, in the middle of Scotland's worst air disaster, and this brain donor was asking, 'What will we find?' I reckon that he sat and thought hard of stupid questions to ask. In order to wind people up.

Once on the trucks, we moved slowly through the town. There were police vans, army trucks and emergency vehicles spilling on to all the very small lanes and causing chaos so the drive took almost 50 minutes, which was in almost complete silence. All I can remember is thinking: 'What does a dead body look like?' Then all I can remember thinking is: 'I don't want to find out, thank you very much.' The truck came to a halt beside a small gate and a couple of trees and we all jumped off the tailgate. The boss and platoon sergeant were discussing map-reading while we stood around either smoking or jumping up and down to try and stay warm.

The only topic of discussion was our length of stay at Lockerbie. Some were saying at least a month. Rumour control had started already!

'Everyone shut up and listen in,' the boss shouted. 'We'll be moving in line formation, keep close and tight.'

'Any questions?' asked the sergeant.

We set off that cold, damp December morning not knowing what to expect. Hour after hour we trudged through fields, over fences and hedges, but we found nothing. Every hour we stopped for a short break and reported back to the incident headquarters. The signaller had told us that 259 passengers had died and I realised then that we had some very grim tasks ahead of us. At lunchtime we loaded back on to the trucks and drove back to the primary school for some hot food. The school was crammed with different emergency services: there were over 1,000 policemen and 600 military personnel drafted in to assist, as well as another four busloads from the RHF who had been sent from Edinburgh. I was told the Salvation Army had set up special phone lines for us. My family were expecting me home that day so I had to phone home and, as I dialled the number, I realised Christmas was only two days away.

'Hello, Mum, it's me,' I said. 'I don't know when I'll be home, I'm at Lockerbie.'

My mother started crying, not because of Lockerbie, but because Christmas was so near and I didn't know when I'd be home. I made a lame excuse about people wanting to use the phone and hung up. I felt sorry for the married guys with kids, but it's all part of the job.

I returned to the canteen and watched the news. I found out that 17 local people had also gone missing in the area where the fuselage had impacted. Back on the trucks we headed to an area much closer to the town and started searching again. The only difference was that this time we now had several police officers with us. By early afternoon it started to rain and the weather matched the mood of the day.

Helicopters continually buzzed low overhead as they had started bringing the bodies into the temporary mortuary at the town hall. We carried on searching the fields and gullies and we found lots of wreckage and debris from the aircraft. I found a Christmas present from the crash in a stream, I lifted it from the water and placed it on the bank. The platoon sergeant came running over: 'Fucking keep your hands to yourself, Donnan!' he screamed, spitting all over me. That really pissed me off. I wanted to punch his face in, but I knew he would kill me. I lifted the present out of respect for whoever it had belonged to, nothing else.

Darkness came quickly and once again we headed back to the school. During meals our padre came round asking how everyone was; he had been out on the ground and witnessed some of the horrors himself. He was well respected within the regiment and always had the Jocks' interest at heart. I noticed a couple of senior blokes come in, some were in tears and white with the shock of what they had just seen. I was glad that we hadn't found any bodies that day as I just didn't know how I could cope. The second night was spent sleeping on the gym floor, along with a few hundred other people. The Sally Army dished out free cigarettes to all the smokers and while they proceeded to smoke themselves to death, I crawled inside my sleeping bag and shut out the world.

Next morning, after breakfast, we had to report to one of the classrooms for a briefing by the platoon commander. As I walked into the room I was given a pair of Marigold gloves – no prizes for guessing why we were given these. At the briefing we were told that any bodies we found were not to be moved. Firstly the police would be informed, then photographs would be taken and any possessions recorded. Our job was to load the bodies into bags and on to the waiting helicopters.

We had been tasked to Tundergarth. From the news on TV I knew this was the area where the cockpit lay in a field like a wounded animal.

'Any questions?' asked the boss.

No one uttered a word, there was nothing to say, nothing that we didn't fucking know already. The drive was very quick and as I jumped off the truck, I realised that we were being filmed by TV cameras. I nipped behind a stone wall for a quick piss and as I finished they were actually filming me. I then let loose with a chorus of expletives that any squaddie would have been proud of. The cameraman was last seen running towards his Land Rover.

I crossed the road and into the field where the cockpit lay. The first thing that struck me was the sheer size of this monster. As I got closer my eyes fixed on what looked like an arm; it was, in fact, a body with no legs. The man had been ripped apart with the force of the metal but he still had his white shirt and badges of rank on his shoulders. It looked so unreal, he looked like a waxwork dummy. Yes, that's it, they were dummies, weren't they?

I stood and stood amidst the twisted metal and the miles of aircraft wires, the stench of aviation fuel and dead people. I found a dismembered air stewardess still strapped in her seat. She was still in the crash position that you have to adopt when the aircraft is going down. I remember thinking that it hadn't done her any good. Just to the left was someone, I say someone because they had no face. The smell of death everywhere made me sick.

The cameras filmed me as I was doubled over with my mate patting me on the back. Today, as I write this book, I cannot begin to describe the horrors that we all faced that day. I search my mind and I picture the scene, as I have a million times before. I know that part of me was angry that people could do this to each other and the sheer madness of it all. Another part of me was sad, very sad that innocent people like you and me could be killed in this terrible way. I never prayed before, but that day I prayed for everyone, the army included! Revenge, killing, death; all I can say is waste, madness, sheer stupidity.

We were then split into small groups and sent to search the forests behind the cockpit area, along with 20 police officers. We came across six other bodies that we could not move as forensic wanted to photograph them in position. They were all twisted and naked as the G-force had ripped the clothes from their backs. We moved through the forest hardly speaking to each other, the only time we stopped was to help a policeman who collapsed with the strain. Tempers started to flare when our group got lost in the woods. We headed back to the church in Tundergarth to get warmed through and to have a brew.

The Salvation Army had set up a small food wagon and provided us with tea and hot food, although no one had an appetite. Inside the church were police, army and mountain-rescue teams and the fire brigade. The church had a huge Christmas tree in the corner and decorations on the walls and ceiling. The minister came through and chatted to us, giving us moral support and listening to anything we had to say. He then went over and started playing the organ; the atmosphere changed instantly. Everyone was tired and sombre, a lot of us broke down in tears, others sat quietly with their own thoughts. That afternoon we returned to the fields to shift yet more bodies and look for any debris. At 1700 hours we headed back to the school for dinner. Most of us couldn't eat, we all sat drinking tea in silence.

One of the regiment's most senior warrant officers wandered over, pulled out a chair and sat beside us. He asked how we were coping and told us that things were not really that bad. We all looked at each other, astounded. If this had been someone else he would have been decked on the spot. He talked more bullshit for a couple of minutes, then he said: 'Don't worry about lifting the bodies, just pretend it's bits of chicken.' I couldn't believe it.

I've heard some bullshit in my time but that was unreal, the guy was deadly serious, which was even more frightening. I got up and went outside for some fresh air and counted to ten very slowly. Our third night in Lockerbie was spent on the gym floor in a sleeping bag and I crashed out in seconds.

Next morning, I crawled out of my sleeping bag and the first thing that hit me was the smell, our combats stank. We had been in the same clothes for three days and had been lifting bits and pieces of bodies and I couldn't even remember when I last had a wash. Then I remembered it was Christmas Eve, as if that made any fucking difference.

The strain was showing on everyone, no laughing, no jokes, just tired-looking people haunted by the last few days' events. We all wanted to go home and hoped to wake up to find that this was nothing more than a bad dream. After a briefing, we spent the first hour in the Sherwood Crescent area, sifting through the rubble. This was a huge crater, almost 30 feet deep, where houses had once stood, but everything had been destroyed by the impact of the fuselage of the aircraft. We then boarded trucks and headed for the Tundergarth area. This time we were given the job of standing guard over some bodies, apparently ghouls had travelled to the area and were stealing belongings. I spent the next two hours standing guard over two bodies in a field. What a way to spend Christmas Eve.

At lunchtime a replacement appeared and told me to head over to the trucks; we clambered on and headed back to the school. The company commander stood waiting as we arrived, we were then told to form up in three ranks.

'Good news. Firstly, coaches will be here in 20 minutes to take us back to camp and, secondly, we are going straight on leave once the kit is sorted out. Get your sleeping bags and be back here at 1400 hours,' he said.

It was great news and we all cheered up immediately. Once on the bus, we all sat down and the boss told us how well we worked together and how proud he was of us all. Someone muttered: 'Save the bullshit for the mess and get the fucking bus going.' The boss carried on talking and ignored the comments. This was the first instance of how Lockerbie had affected us all in some way, as if this had been any other situation, the culprit would have been charged with insubordination. Within minutes we were all sleeping as the coach headed back to the camp in Edinburgh.

Once inside the camp, we repacked our kit and sorted out travel warrants to get us back home. The army didn't give us any extra leave, even though we missed a couple of days – that's gratitude for you. I searched out the company colour sergeant who was responsible for the issue of clothing and stores. My combats were bloodstained and I wanted to exchange them for a new set. I found the colour sergeant in the storeroom. He was a very nasty man.

'Colour, I was wondering if I could . . .' I said.

'No, you fucking can't,' he said, cutting me off. 'Now fuck off!' he shouted.

I thought, 'That's really fucking charming that is, the army really knows how to look after its own.'

I grabbed my bag and headed to the city centre to catch the train home. It was good to be out of uniform and away from the arseholes in the regiment. Once in Edinburgh all I could see were hundreds of Christmas shoppers. I was shocked to see that everything was going on as normal. I wanted to shake people and tell them about Lockerbie. How could they smile and be happy, how dare they prepare to celebrate Christmas after what had happened? I was pissed off, so I went for a few beers.

I got home in the early evening and my family were pleased to see me. I was tired and didn't want to speak to anyone. So I went straight to my room and into bed.

Next morning was Christmas Day. My younger sisters were very excited and dragged me out of bed to open my presents. Grudgingly I opened them and wished everyone a Merry Christmas and then went back to bed. I didn't feel like celebrating, I wanted time alone. My family were having dinner at a friend's house and I upset everyone by refusing to attend. Once they left I sat and looked through all the newspapers. Lockerbie had been the headline story for the past few days. I picked up the *Daily Record* and inside were 30 pictures of victims and I immediately recognised one as a body I helped move. That's when it really hit me and I started to cry. My thoughts were confused and I sat there unable to describe my feelings. I became angry, then sad and then angry again. I decided to get drunk, so that's what I did. A full bottle of Southern Comfort helped dull the senses.

On Boxing Day I watched the news as my commanding officer commented: 'They responded magnificently to a gruesome task. Many of them have never seen a dead body before, but they all carried out the task well.' He carried on by saying: 'Many people run down teenagers of today, but you should have seen the 18- and 19-year-old Fusiliers at Lockerbie. They were something to be proud of.'

My first thought was: 'How can you do a task like that, and then be told you have done it well?' My mind raced back to Lockerbie Primary School and the church where everyone sat in tears. Yes, we responded fucking magnificently, didn't we? I then remembered what the platoon sergeant said some weeks back that all officers were 'mentally retarded pondlife'. I was beginning to understand what he meant.

The *Daily Record* carried a story headlined MUCH WORSE THAN A BATTLEFIELD. It was about a young squaddie who broke down to a reporter and said: 'They trained us for what we might see in a war, but you can't believe what this unimaginable destruction is doing to us.' Yes, we responded magnificently, didn't we?

The next couple of days passed in a drunken blur. I'd meet up with a couple of army mates who lived close by and then we'd all get very pissed. On one of our drinking sessions we overheard a man repeating a very sick joke about Lockerbie and it really annoyed us, so my mate punched him off the bar stool and he dropped to the floor then I ran forward and kicked him in the head, and shouted that he was a cunt. As I write these words I am ashamed of what I did that day. We all wanted to look hard in front of each other, it was a macho squaddie thing. We took all our anger out on this poor guy.

It was about this time I had my first nightmare, which was a frightening experience. I dreamt that I was on the aircraft as it came screaming towards earth but somehow I survived and lay screaming for someone to help us all before we died, but no one came. I then crawled from the wreckage and climbed up a tree. It was at that point I woke up. At the time I thought it was strange, but I didn't tell anyone about my nightmares. Often I would get out of bed and go for a long walk and try to make sense of the last few weeks, but it always eluded me.

My mother commented a few times on the amount I was drinking and that I was never in the house and if I was, then I was so drunk I couldn't speak. 'Yeah, yeah, yeah,' I thought, 'I am fucking fine.' I was 17 and acting like an arsehole, but who cares?

My ten days' leave passed very quickly and I returned to the barracks on 5 January 1989. I collected my kit from the stores and settled into my old room and found it was good to see a few mates again. Lockerbie was never mentioned by anyone, it seemed to be a touchy subject for a few people.

The next two days were spent scrubbing the barracks ready to hand it over to the next regiment. It was an exciting time as we packed kit and prepared for our posting to outside Cambridge. In just over a year's time the whole regiment would be heading to Belize, Central America, for a six-month jungle tour, so this coming year would be spent training hard and learning jungle tactics. I was really looking forward to the next couple of years. I had joined the army to travel and, hopefully, to see the world and I wanted to get stuck straight into my job.

The day before we were leaving for Cambridge, the company commander called for a room inspection. All my kit was packed into huge boxes for the move, so I gutted the room and polished all the windows. As the major and my platoon sergeant neared my room I stood at attention; he walked in and asked my name.

'24823178 Donnan, sir.'

The major checked under my bed for dust and then down behind the radiator. My heart stopped as he found something; a pen had been painted on to the radiator some years before. He managed to break it free and asked me what it was. Before I could answer he cut in: 'You're not paying attention to detail, get a fucking grip, Donnan.'

The sergeant-major then had his turn: 'Don't eyeball me when I'm talking to you!'

'Yes, sir!' I shouted.

He walked out of the room and then turned and came back in: 'Corporal, get this man over to the jail right now.'

So I was doubled-marched over to the guardroom and spent the afternoon doing press-ups, polishing anything that needed it – windows, floors, desks, boots – and making tea for the fat lazy bastards who worked there. I was shocked that such a big punishment was given out for nothing but, as I later learned, that is the army way. I actually thought Jeremy Beadle was going to jump out and say it was a wind-up. I was eventually released back to my platoon feeling tired and pissed off. It was my first brush with authority, but it certainly would not be the last.

3. Cambridge

In late January we boarded several coaches and headed south to Cambridge. The journey was a good laugh, people slagging each other off, but I just sat and listened. Some of the senior blokes were having a good moan about the fact we were being posted to England although I didn't see that it mattered very much. We arrived at Oakington Barracks late at night and it looked like a concentration camp. It had been a Second World War airfield and it was in the middle of nowhere.

I was given a room with eight other squaddies, most of whom were all senior blokes. It felt a bit like my first day at school and I realised that I was still very much the new guy or 'red arse'. Over the next couple of days we settled in and unpacked all our kit into lockers and as I was the red arse, I had plenty of menial tasks to get on with. Every morning we had block jobs to do, ranging from mopping the toilets to dusting the room and, in theory, everybody mucks in, but in reality I had to do them all myself, because, as I was often reminded, I had been in only 'five minutes'. A lot of the older blokes would not even speak to me, unless it was to give me a hard time for something I'd done wrong. Everyone who joins the army is treated like that and I knew it would pass in time.

That first weekend, six or seven old sweats came into the room when they were pissed and tipped me out of bed and on to the floor. I could hear someone getting the shit kicked out of them in the corridor and I was crapping myself.

'Get fucking over here, you!' one of them said nastily. As I slowly walked towards him I could smell the drink. I wanted to run, but I knew I had to face this. In the middle of the room was a small bedside locker. 'Bend over the locker, you wanker.'

I really didn't know what was going to happen. At one point I thought he was going to shag me. Reluctantly, I leaned over the locker and waited. One of them stepped forward and sank his teeth into the cheeks of my arse. He bit hard and held for ages. I screamed as it was so painful. This was the initiation ritual I'd heard about in Edinburgh but I could scarcely believe the agony. After this I was accepted a bit more – strange or what?

The following week we started our preliminary jungle training and we received several lectures on the history of Belize. Then we would change into PT kit and go for a six- or seven-mile run. I really enjoyed the training and settled down very well. During this period I struck up a firm friendship with a guy called Craig Bryan. His background was not dissimilar to my own and we both shared a very strange, black sense of humour. He had joined the regiment only four months before me. Weekends would come and we would head into town and get very drunk.

One weekend we waited for a taxi outside the main gate, as it appeared, two old sweats ran over and tried to get in the car with us. It turned out the taxi wasn't for any of us and we climbed back out. As the car pulled away, one of them started on Craig.

'Who the fuck do you think you are?'

'I'm sorry, mate. Just leave it, eh?' Craig was saying.

'No, I fucking won't. Do you know who I am?'

My mate was nearly 16 stone and would have been a match for most of the regiment. Anyway, this Glasgow hard man was really pushing for a fight.

'Let's fucking go for it, you and me.'

Craig slipped off his jacket and handed it to me, then casually leaned over and knocked the other guy out, apologised, then climbed into our waiting taxi. I was impressed.

Army life consists of 20 per cent activity and 80 per cent boredom. It was very different from the training depot; here you could skive all day if you wanted. Some days we got up, changed into uniform and then lay in bed all morning, then we went to lunch and then lay about again. I hated this aspect of life in the battalion, everything was so negative. In the infantry, if you're doing nothing then it is a good day, because you could be out in the pissing rain humphing an 84mm anti-tank weapon across Otterburn. So, if you're not doing anything then it's more positive.

Training carried on in stops and starts. One of the NCOs (non-commissioned officers) opened a small cupboard and found a Jock lying sleeping wrapped in a carpet; he'd been in there all day. Several squaddies were caught having a fly wank in the toilets.

I took part in a week-long signals course which was all about antennae, battle codes and call signs. I hated it and told them so but it made no difference. At the final exam I was careful not to score high marks as it this would mean a posting to a signals platoon, which I didn't want.

The regiment was awarded with the Wilkinson Sword of Honour for its part in the Lockerbie air disaster. The citation said:

> The 1st Battalion the Royal Highland Fusiliers are based in Edinburgh. On 21 December 1988, the battalion was looking forward to Christmas leave when they heard on the radio of the Lockerbie air disaster. Elements of the battalion immediately deployed to the area and the scale of the disaster became apparent. The initial sub-units at the primary site

were soon aiding the local community of Lockerbie and assisting with the recovery of the dead. Thereafter, the battalion's involvement increased as other organisations found it hard to cope with the tragedy. Many of the young soldiers were confronted with situations beyond imagination but continued selflessly with their primary task of recovering the bodies dispersed over a wide area. The conduct of the soldiers during this traumatic period demonstrated the commitment and the team spirit of the battalion and, above all, was a prime example of the professionalism of the army. In February 1989 the battalion moved to Cambridge, where they not only established a close relationship with their new neighbours but also maintained their bond with Lockerbie by continuing their active support for charities linked with the disaster.

We were pleased that someone had recognised our hard work at Lockerbie, but it wasn't good enough. This was the only time that Lockerbie was ever mentioned within the battalion, even though a lot of soldiers were still struggling to come to terms with what they had seen. I was still having nightmares and mood swings, but I was scared to speak to the doctor as I didn't want to seem weak. In my own case I thought this was normal and that it would pass in time. As for the army top brass, they either didn't know or didn't care.

In March that year we took part in a huge defence exercise down on Salisbury Plain. We had an exchange platoon sergeant from New Zealand who was a Maori. Sergeant Hu was a very hard man with plenty of soldiering experience, but all his years in the army never prepared him for Salisbury Plain in the winter. At one point he was wearing three jumpers and three jackets and a towel round his head to keep warm.

I had been trying to dig in for two days and had got down about a foot. I was moved to four different locations. The ground was so hard with frost and rock that nearly 50 soldiers went down with hypothermia and eventually the exercise was scrapped.

Back in camp that night, while everyone was sleeping, I could hear someone creeping round the room. When I looked across at the other bed space, I was shocked to see Les standing over Alan's bed with a shovel, about to smash him over the head with it.

'What the fuck are you on?' I asked stupidly.

'I'm gonnae kill this bastard,' Les said.

It turned out that Alan had been giving Les a hard time on exercise and Les had got pissed and now wanted revenge. I told him that maybe it wasn't such a good idea, unless he wanted to be locked up for a long time. He agreed, and I put his shovel in my locker. I climbed into bed and made a mental note never to annoy Les.

Over the next month I was sent on a civilian first-aid course run by the St John's Ambulance Brigade in Cambridge. I learned everything about first aid at an advanced level and I really enjoyed the course. On the final day I was tested by a doctor, both written and practical tests; I came second on the course, so I was chuffed.

Back at the battalion I was now training very hard and running about 100 miles a week. I had become totally 'army barmy', I loved the job and the life and, as far as I was con-cerned, I would stay in the army for life. My secret ambition was to transfer to the Army Air Corps and train to be a helicopter pilot.

One night after training, I climbed into bed knackered. At about four in the morning the fire alarm sounded so I jumped up and put my tracksuit bottoms on and we all scrambled outside the building, thinking it was a normal fire practice. Suddenly the platoon corporals appeared, even the married ones, and I was grabbed and then blindfolded and ordered to stand still. I could hear people shouting: 'What the fuck's going on?'

'Shut the fuck up and don't fucking move,' the NCOs screamed.

My hands were tied and someone started dragging me across the tarmac. I tried to resist and was punched on the jaw. 'You bastard!' I shouted. Again I was punched, this time on the head so I decided to keep my mouth shut. After about 20 minutes' walking, I was pushed face down into the mud. For the next hour I could hear the screams of my mates as they were systematically tortured and then questioned. Every ten minutes an NCO would walk along the line and give us a good kick on the head. I remember from training that all we had to answer was the big four: name, rank, number and date of birth but from what I could hear, nearly everyone had cracked and given more information than they should have. The training team were using all the tricks of the trade, like taking the spare wheel from a Land Rover and pushing it against your head whilst nearby a Jeep would start its engine. They would ask a couple of questions and if you didn't answer then they would scream and shout that the Land Rover was about to drive over your head. It was amazing just how many of us happily informed the 'enemy' everything that they needed to know. I was glad it wasn't for real or we'd all be fucked.

After the instructors got bored at kicking the shit out of us, we were driven to an airfield 30 miles away. It was now early afternoon and I was starving and pissed off.

'Right, gather round here,' shouted the boss. We all ran over, waiting to see what was going on. 'Okay, lads, it's lunchtime, so listen in carefully,' said Captain Knox, our training officer. I was paired off with my mate Craig. An NCO led us over to a small tree, underneath the tree was our lunch – a fucking rabbit and a pigeon, and a carrot and an onion. I was well pissed off as I didn't like meat at the best of times. We sat down, split the carrot in half and munched away and we had a good moan about our starter. Craig skinned the rabbit and plucked the skinniest pigeon that I've ever had the misfortune to meet; by the looks of things it was better off dead. About two hours later I was holding a black and charred object that was once a bird. It looked disgusting but I was so hungry I tried a bite and found it tasted like burnt rubber, I decided to starve for the rest of the day.

Our next task was to build a raft and paddle out to an island in the middle of a small lake. This was fairly easy as we had plenty of kit lying around. We tied oil drums together with rope, lashed planks of wood on as a platform, so it worked quite well. Unknown to us, however, the NCOs had sabotaged them all and we sank halfway over to the island. We dragged ourselves back to the shore and gathered round two of the instructors who were very dry. They both knew what we had in mind, so they ran and jumped in before we could grab them.

Back at camp, we all headed straight to the cookhouse for some decent food – if you could call it that. We also found out that one bloke, who was a complete headcase and who was universally known as 'Mad Dog', was on the run somewhere in Cambridge. It turned out that when we'd all been dragged from our beds that morning, Mad Dog realised something strange was going on, so he jumped out of the window and started running while we stood and watched as he disappeared into the distance. It was quite funny and the training team were well pissed off. After dinner I headed back to the block for a shower and an early night as I was shattered. I went to bed just after nine and quickly fell asleep. The next thing I remember was a blow to the face, I opened my eyes just to make sure it was real, again I was punched on the nose and my eyes were watering, I could taste blood.

'Get fucking up, me and you, outside now!' said the voice. I grabbed my tracksuit and went outside the block. In the light I recognised my attacker as an arsehole from 6 Platoon, who obviously disliked me. We started punching into each other and then one of his mates jumped out from behind a wall. I didn't stand a chance. I ended up on the ground clutching my ribs, three of which were cracked, my nose was broken and my face was a mass of blood. I lay outside for a while, I was still in shock and could hardly move. Eventually I got up and went inside the block and back to my bed.

At about 0600 hours the orderly sergeant woke everyone up, by whatever means handy. Corporal Smith had a metal dustbin lid which he would strike with a brush handle, very fucking annoying indeed, it put everyone in a bad mood for the day. 'Re – veille, re – veille,' he would sing at the top of his voice. I think I could have quite easily choked the cheery, annoying bastard to death, just for some peace and quiet.

I looked at my face in the mirror, it was not a pretty sight.

After breakfast the orderly sergeant came looking for me as the two Jocks who had given me a kicking had also gone AWOL (absent without leave). When he saw me he said: 'Get over to the medical centre and see the doc.'

At the med centre I was cleaned up and given a once-over by the doctor, my nose was broken and my ribs cracked and my ego was dented. On the way out, the clerk shouted me back into his office: 'Report straight to the company sergeant-major's office.'

'Yes, sir,' I replied, trying hard to think if I had done anything wrong.

It was one of those days that went from bad to really fucking shite. I was well pissed off and feeling sorry for myself. Before I marched into the company office, I checked my uniform, just to make sure I was smart enough as I couldn't face a bollocking for having a button undone or for any other stupid reason.

'Stand over there beside the wall,' said the orderly sergeant. I stood against the wall for about 50 minutes, feeling like I was on exhibition. Every now and again someone would appear round the corner and ask what had happened.

'I cut myself shaving, would you believe?' I replied.

'Donnan, march in here!' shouted the sergeant-major in his best pissed-off voice. I marched in and halted in front of his desk. 'What happened last night outside the block?' So I explained everything once again to the sergeant-major. 'You have really fucking annoyed me, Donnan,' he said. I couldn't believe what I was hearing. I had ten shades of shit kicked out of me and I was getting a hard time about it. 'You went straight back to bed after what happened, it should have been reported immediately, you could have died in your bed, Donnan.' I was now very pissed off and tried to explain that I could hardly walk, but I was told to shut up. 'Take this man to the jail!' he shouted.

Almost immediately a small lance-corporal came running into the office, screaming at the top of his voice. 'Get outside and stand at attention. Go to the pace I call out, by the left, quick march!' He was in a frenzy. I was bewildered, it was quite funny at the time, so I was doubled to the guardroom by this nasty little man. Once inside the jail the provost staff wanted to know what I had done so they could arrange a suitable punishment for me.

'Well?' said the provost corporal.

'I got a kicking last night, and because I didn't report it immediately, the sergeant-major sent me down here,' I mumbled. They looked at each other, one of them made a face.

'Who is your sergeant-major?'

'Sergeant-Major Blackwood, staff.'

'Get through the back and start sweeping up,' I was told.

So I spent the whole day in the guardroom doing menial tasks. I never really got a hard time, I think the provost staff were as confused as I was. Afterwards, I went straight to the NAAFI (the canteen) for a few beers. If life is shit, get pissed and have a good moan, it sometimes helps!

Next morning I had more bad news: I was to go on yet another signals course, for four weeks this time. I was not fucking happy, if I had wanted to be a signaller I would have joined the Royal Signals. I protested to my platoon sergeant, his reply was: 'My heart pumps purple pish, now fuck off!' So the next four weeks were spent learning about the setting up of command posts, installing radios in vehicles and antennas. I hated every minute of it, but I passed the course and was now a regimental signaller.

I was still training very hard in my spare time as I was determined to get a transfer to the army air corps. All I wanted was a couple of years' experience with an infantry regiment and then, hopefully, I might be accepted on the pilots' course. We had an air corps' squadron based on our camp, and at weekends I would hang around trying to chat to the pilots and hoping to be allowed a flight with them.

Back at the platoon we started intensive training for the inter-section competition called the Rowallan Targe. This was a route march of a hundred miles to be undertaken in teams of eight and our objective was to get around the route in the fastest time. Days would be spent brushing up on first aid, NBC (nuclear–biological–chemical) warfare, map reading and patrol skills. Every morning we would run seven or eight miles and then after lunch it would be over to the gym for a beasting. These periods were very intense but we were learning a lot. I loved the training and the hard work.

I had settled in quite well and was trying hard to put Lockerbie to the back of my mind and I wasn't the only one. It was still a taboo subject and had never been mentioned within the regiment; perhaps we didn't want to realise just how much it had affected us, perhaps we were just fucking scared. Big, tough soldiers we were, but we were still human – sometimes. At weekends we would head into the town and get drunk out of our minds, fights would start, civvies would get the shit kicked out of them, usually for no reason other than just being there. I think so many of us were bottling up feelings and this was a stupid way of getting some anger out of your system.

Most of the regiment were absolutely nuts. Every Monday morning there would be 20 or 30 men being hauled up in front of the CO after having drunk far too much over the weekend and done something stupid. It amazed me that no one bothered to find out why.

On the morning of the competition, we boarded four-tonners and headed to Otterburn training area. As usual, it was pishing down – the army had a knack of picking the most barren and windswept shitholes for training areas, and this was no exception. We loaded up our rucksacks and checked our kit. My kit weighed 100lbs and I also carried a radio, I felt like a donkey. Eight of us set off at a fairly steady pace and quickly covered the ten miles to the first stand, here we completed a basic first-aid test, then it was rucksacks on and we were given our next checkpoint. After a few miles I became the lead scout. Walking near the road, I noticed an adder in front of me so, using the barrel of my weapon, I picked it up and, for some unknown reason, I hurled it in the air; it landed with a heavy thud on the road. Seeing a chance to wind up a few people, I declared that I had broken the snake's back.

'So you have,' Davey said, examining the reptile.

'Drop this on it,' Les said, carrying a huge rock which he promptly dropped on the snake.

'Yeah!' we were all cheering, as if it was something of which to be proud. Someone stabbed it with a knife and kicked it. When I think of this incident now, I wonder if we were all trying to prove something to each other. We marched on and on.

At the next checkpoint we had a signals test, again we all passed. We stopped for a scoff and changed our socks. My feet had blisters the size of golf balls on them, it was agony. One of the new guys had decided to wear army-issue drill socks which were made of pure nylon. His feet were bleeding and the skin was coming off in sheets. The commander punched him on the face for being such a stupid wanker; nothing like a punch on the face to help sore feet. I overheard the commander telling an officer about the snake's back being broken. The officer was laughing but the commander didn't know why.

Once again we set off to another checkpoint. We were all in agony and the pace had slowed right down. After dark we stopped for a brew and a short rest and as we drank tea we moaned about life, army boots and, in particular, 'army fucking exercises' – which were a killer. Then we fell asleep.

Three hours later I woke up because it was freezing. I looked at my watch in disbelief. It was pitch-dark and I was the only one awake. I contemplated going back to sleep, but I was so cold I wanted to be up and moving. The commander nearly had a heart attack when I told him we had all fallen asleep. We thought it was funny – he didn't.

We carried on marching through the night and my body was in pain and I was staggering with fatigue and the weight of my kit. At dawn we neared the next checkpoint which was 1,500 feet up a hill. I was picked to accompany the commander to the checkpoint while the others waited under a small bridge. It took over an hour to get there. At the checkpoint we met an officer who told us our task was 20 miles away and that we had to carry out a close-target reconnaissance of a small farm.

Back at the bridge we had a quick breakfast and listened to the commander as he dished out his orders, which consisted of patrol formations and actions on how we would react as a patrol to certain situations. I was given two extra weapons to carry as some of the new guys couldn't handle the pace. My extra training was helping me, I was knackered but I would never give in. After five miles the pace was very slow and we were in the middle of nowhere. We dived for cover as we heard a lorry approach us but found it was a civilian furniture removals truck. The patrol second in command ran on to the road and waved the truck down. He made a deal with the driver to drive us to the farm for £15. We climbed in the truck and enjoyed the rest. This was totally against the rules – if anyone had seen us getting out of the truck then we'd be fucked.

Ten hours later we had won the competition and no one ever found out why. We had cheated and there was no doubt about that. We guessed, however, that other sections had done the same thing, but perhaps we were the first to think of it. Army training taught us all about using our initiative, and that's what we were doing – yeah, that sounded good. It is amazing what you can justify when you put your mind to it.

A week later our section proudly posed for a photograph and collected the regimental shield. Later that afternoon we packed our kit and went on summer leave, having been given an extra day because we had worked so hard and won the competition. I spent my leave cycling around the fens of East Anglia, a very relaxing break. The horrors of what I witnessed at Lockerbie still deeply troubled me and I just didn't want to be around people who weren't connected to the army as I felt that they just wouldn't understand how I felt. I was now 18 and had no idea how to handle what I had seen.

After leave, it was good to see my mates again. We unpacked our kit and settled back into routine very quickly. Training for Belize started almost straightaway, with several lectures on jungle warfare. About 20 officers and NCOs had been sent to Borneo to take part in the jungle-warfare instructors' course and they would then pass on the necessary skills to us once we reached Belize.

One night after training, the door burst open and several unknown faces came racing into our billet. 'Stand by your beds!' shouted the officer. We all stood up and wandered over to our respective bed spaces. I waited and waited, we were all really pissed off. Every now and again we would be told to 'shut the fuck up'.

After nearly two hours of standing at attention, a female officer with the Royal Military Police appeared. She had a dog with her. 'Open your lockers and move away from them,' she told us. I watched as this mucky, fucking beast sniffed and crawled its way over my neatly pressed kit. It took me a couple of minutes to realise that this was a drugs raid then I was shocked, disgusted even. I had never witnessed any drug-taking since I joined the army, in fact, I had never even heard of drugs being mentioned and I had just presumed no one ever touched them. I was wrong.

I think about twenty soldiers were caught with drugs inside their lockers. On average, the military police expect to catch three or four at most within an infantry regiment. I wondered if this was anything to do with Lockerbie, people trying to blot things out of their minds.

Next morning I was picked at random by the military police to take part in a drugs test. I gave them a urine sample and thought the matter was over.

'Can you come with me, please?' The officer ushered me into a small room. 'Sit down, Donnan,' he said coldly.

'I'd rather stand, sir.'

'I'm telling you to sit down.' I pulled a seat over and sat beside his desk.

'I am Lieutenant Jones of the Royal Military Police investigating alleged drug misuse within your regiment, do you understand?'

'Yes, sir.'

'Right. I have evidence here which states that you and several others – who cannot be named – smoked a joint in your billet on 23 March 1989.'

'Sir, I have never even smoked a cigarette in my life,' I protested.

'Well, I have written statements here.'

'I don't even know what drugs look like, sir.'

e was bullshitting. I had never touched drugs in my
ow what you've been up to, Donnan.' I realised that
bing in the dark, trying his luck, just to see if anyone
under his interview technique. He was trying to
work us against each other, but I had nothing to hide. I started
laughing at the evidence and told him it was all bullshit.

'Do you think it's funny?' he asked, fuming.

'Yes, sir,' I told him.

That was a mistake. He kept me in the interview room for
two hours before, eventually, letting me go saying that he was
'just checking'.

On my way over to the cookhouse I met Craig who was
equally pissed off. It didn't seem fair that any one of us could be
pulled in and questioned with evidence that was lies. 'We could
always phone the newspapers,' I suggested.

'Good idea,' Craig said.

After dinner, we went straight to the NAAFI to buy a
newspaper. After I had bought a copy of *The Sun*, Craig and I
decided to go to the town and the privacy of a call box. I phoned
the newspaper and asked to speak to a reporter. I explained that
I was a serving soldier with the British Army and no names
could be mentioned and I also told him that the public should
be aware of what was going on inside the army. He agreed that
we should talk.

Two hours later we met and I grassed on my beloved army.
Next day it made front-page news and the commanding officer
was furious. He called the whole regiment to the parade square
and he promised he would find the source and that 'heads will
roll'. I was shitting myself. Next morning, after roll-call, I was
summoned to the platoon sergeant's office. Panic set in; I knew
he would fill me in on the spot if he suspected anything.

'Am I a nasty bastard, Donnan?'

'No, Sergeant,' I lied.

'Do you want me to be?' he asked.

'No, Sergeant,' I shouted, making sure he could hear me.

'I've heard a rumour that you tipped off the newspaper.'

Oh, fuck, I was flapping good style now. 'No. I don't know anything about it,' I said, trying to play it down.

He closed the office door then, with both hands, he grabbed my neck and pulled me towards him. 'If you or anybody else fucks me about, you're for the high jump. Do you understand?'

'Yes, Sergeant,' I said, nearly in tears. This guy was a complete mental bastard. I had no doubt he could make my life a misery. I made a vow on the spot never to be such an arsehole again.

The following day we travelled to Salisbury Plain for a jungle-training exercise. I wondered how they were going to work that one out. We thought maybe they had hired Twentieth-Century Fox to recreate a jungle scene for us, but no, it was normal, boring, pissing-wet Salisbury Plain. We had to pretend we were in the jungle – or so the instructors told us – but most of the time was spent standing around waiting for something to happen. The highlight of the exercise was our new ration packs which now contained more chocolate than ever.

Back in camp we were issued with our new jungle light-weights and a pair of boots; it was like Christmas all over again. I had spent so much time learning about the jungle and Belize that I was desperate to get there and get stuck in. The next year or so would be full of hard work and adventure and we were all excited.

Another time, we had an exchange visit to RAF Honington for a day; we were split into groups of six and given a guide. My host for the day was Flight-Lieutenant John Peters, the Tornado pilot who later became famous during the Gulf War. We were shown around the flight line and inside the control tower then, after lunch, we had our very own Tornado to play with. It was at times like this I wished that I'd stuck at my school work and gained some decent results – if I had then maybe I could have been a fighter pilot.

Back at camp I was given a message to go and see the company commander. 'Oh, fuck,' I thought. I was worried that maybe word had got back to him about the newspapers.

'Come in, Donnan,' said the major. 'Right, go and pack your kit, we are going to take part in the ambulance strike.' I didn't know if he meant we would be helping the people on strike or what. In fact I didn't even know there was a strike on – after all, I was just a grunt.

We boarded a coach that took us to Welwyn Garden City, where our new home was the police headquarters. Six of us shared a police flat and as I was the only private, I got all the shitty jobs. One of the sergeants from another platoon was there and he hated me, but that was all right because the feeling was mutual – very mutual. He was a nasty, evil individual who enjoyed inflicting pain and misery on us lower ranks. The regiment was full of arseholes. It seemed that once you were a sergeant or above, you suddenly became a fully-fledged arsehole. We reckoned there was a secret course where they would go and learn how to become complete bastards; it was something they were all good at.

One afternoon when I was inside the police operations room, I was standing talking to a young WPC when Sergeant Nasty entered.

'Donnan, move your fucking arse right now and get the fucking tea, you wanker!'

The policewoman looked on in disbelief. I was fucking unhappy, so, as I made his tea, I thought, 'I'll show the cunt,' and I filled half his cup with piss. 'Here you go, Sergeant,' I said, handing him the cup.

I watched with great enjoyment as he drank every single drop. This was a major victory for the rest of the lads who hated him too. In fact, it became something of a ritual after that – we always had something to contribute to his tea!

My job was to run the ops room through the night and liaise

with the police control room. I enjoyed it as I was, more or less, left to my own devices. During the day I would train in the gym and then use the police swimming-pool, then after lunch I would train with the police firearms team. I loved it. I made a lot of new friends and who knows, perhaps one day I might join the police.

So, for the next three months, I worked there, doing two weeks on and ten days off. I was practically a civvy again. I was quite sad going back to the RHF, but it was time to deploy to Belize and some new adventures.

4. It's a Jungle Out There

We were the first party to arrive in Belize from the RHF. I can't remember what time it was, except it was fucking dark and raining. I had never seen rain like it. I thought that was just typical. It rained all that night and into the next morning, apparently it was monsoon season and this was quite normal.

I was part of the pre-advance party, our job being to check and take over equipment from the departing regiment, the Gurkha Rifles. The main body would follow us out in three weeks' time.

Belize was a former colony of British Honduras and it had had a troubled past with the neighbouring country of Guatemala who had refused to recognise British sovereignty. Our job was to help patrol the borders and stem any hostile threats. We were part of a small British garrison along with several Harrier aircraft, a detachment of artillery and armoured reconnaissance vehicles.

Our rooms were in small, round tin huts and although I thought they were crap, I was told this was luxury compared to how the locals lived. The Gurkhas loved it there and took great delight in telling me how many women they had shagged at the local whorehouse. In fact, most of them spent their entire wages in the brothel. After work they would make Gurkha curries over an open fire, drink whisky straight and then go 'jiggy-jiggy' as they called it. At breakfast time they would stagger into camp, get changed and then run eight or nine miles. They had a fearsome reputation within the British Army, and quite rightly so.

My opposite number from the Gurkhas asked me to take part in a ten-kilometre road race which he had arranged. So, ignoring all the rules about acclimatisation, I agreed. Ten minutes after the start I was lying in a ditch, gasping for breath. That was my first lesson about the dangers of heat exhaustion and it wouldn't be my last.

I loved my time with the Gurkhas. I learned a lot about them in the three weeks. They were passionate about the British Army and everything they took part in.

By the time my regiment had arrived I had settled in and was really starting to enjoy being in Belize. When things go well in the army, enjoy it – because it never lasts.

I was pissed off to learn that my first job was 'stagging on' (being on duty) in the ops room. I didn't come all the way to Belize to sit in an ops room all day, I wanted to be out in the jungle doing patrols – at least trying to be a soldier. I explained this to the sergeant-major, but his reply was the usual: 'Fuck off and wind your neck in!' At that point I would have quite willingly swum back to the US rather than spend my time in the ops room. Worse still, my boss was Tommy the Turtle, a walking, talking, sleeping tablet. I didn't want to be sidelined as a signaller, because I felt it was too early on in my career for that. Most signallers were guys who couldn't hack the hard life in a rifle company and I didn't want tarred with the same brush. I explained to the major – who was quite sympathetic – and he promised that he would include me in any patrols, perhaps as a signaller or a medic. That would have to do under the circumstances, but I was still unhappy.

It was at this time I met our new commanding officer, a large, jovial man who looked more like Father Christmas than an army officer. He had a strange habit of punching people; he would walk up beside you then lash out. I thought it was maybe some kind of ritual or something. Apparently the more he liked you, the harder he would punch you – strange.

I started my endless round of ops duty: 12 hours on and 12 off. It was so fucking boring I would usually fall asleep at my desk except during the specific hours when all patrols would call in and give a situation report (sit reps). My job was to take down all the details and record them in a log book. Normally, the Turtle would come in for a chat, usually about radios, then he would start dusting them down and talking about call signs and shit like that, at which point I would stop listening and let him ramble on.

After my stag was finished, I would head straight to the swimming-pool and lie in the sun all day. Most of the time the pool was closed, due to people shitting in it. There was a good reason for this, though: the timings always favoured army families, so this was our way of protesting. At weekends everyone would get shit-faced. If Belize was ever invaded, then the weekend would be the time to do it – no one could walk, never mind stem an invasion threat.

After two weeks I was sent into the jungle on a training course and I loved it. We learned everything about the jungle – what we could eat, how to make basic shelters and, of course, all the relevant tactics. Our instructors cooked snake, iguana, turtle and pigs, then invited us to eat them. The jungle was very hard work, but it was immensely rewarding and I was learning lots of new things every day. At the survival lecture, the instructor could not find any of the turtles, in fact a few of us let them go the night before, trying to save their lives. We didn't want to see them butchered in front of us. I told you we were still human.

Unknown to us, they hadn't wandered very far, one of the officers found them when he was nipping out for a piss. So you can imagine our surprise when he placed them on the six-foot table which was covered in blood from previous reptiles that had been cut up. The poor thing must have known what was about to happen because as soon as it was placed on the table, its head retracted into its shell. We were delighted. The instructor tried everything to get its head out, including tempting it with its favourite leafy food, but it still refused. We were just about cheering. This went on for about 40 minutes, surely the instructor would give in shortly. Wrong! The guy made a small noose out of para cord and placed it over and round the turtle's head and with one hand he pulled its head free, then he chopped it off with a machete. That pissed us off for the rest of the day.

As I boarded a helicopter to take me back to camp, I was determined not to miss out on any time spent in the jungle, or the 'jay' as we called it. I would have quite happily spent my whole six months in the jungle instead of going back to camp.

At the helipad my boss, Tony, stood waiting for me. 'Go and get washed and shaved, you're on stag in 50 minutes.'

'What?' I said, disbelieving what I heard.

'You heard. If you fuck me about, I'll fuck you about.'

The whole time we were in Belize he never once went into the jungle because he was a lazy bastard whereas I had volunteered to go on the course, knowing it was the only way I could get on some patrols. When someone told him that I wanted to be back with my platoon, he deemed this as disloyal to the signals detachment, so this was my punishment, death by signals.

'You can check all the serial numbers tonight after the sit reps,' he said, gloating.

This was extra misery, all because I wanted to be out soldiering instead of playing with radios.

'Do you hear me?' he asked.

'Yes, Corporal,' I replied. 'What a wanker,' I thought. I also thought how much I would like to stamp on his face.

After a night stag I would go straight out by myself on a ten-mile run, then, if it was open, I would go to the pool and swim a mile. I was now more determined than ever to get to the Army Air Corps as a pilot. One morning, after a run, I met my old platoon sergeant, John Kirkland. 'Enjoying signals, are we?' he said, laughing, knowing only too well how much I hated it. 'I'm leading a boat patrol shortly, we need a signaller, fancy it?' he asked.

'Yes, definitely, Sergeant,' I replied, seizing a chance to get away from the Turtle.

'I'll sort it out and then I'll get back to you.'

'Cheers, Sergeant.'

Most of my stags were night duties – yet more punishment – so I never really spent much time with my mates. When I did, we always went into Belize City and got legless as it was always a good laugh. I was really enjoying my time there. We all tried hard to forget about the horrors of Lockerbie, maybe it was the idyllic setting, or the fact we were in another country, it just seemed easier, sometimes.

'Donnan, outside my office at 1400 hours, you're on interviews,' shouted the sergeant-major.

'Yes, sir.'

I thought it would be an interview about my future career within the signals platoon, so I pressed my kit and waited outside the office. I was marched in by the sergeant-major.

'Stand easy, Donnan,' said Major Archibald. 'A number of people have commented on your work and your attitude, Donnan. We feel that you're being held back within this regiment so I am going to recommend you for a commission. When we return to the UK you will take part in Operation Raleigh, then we'll see about getting you into Sandhurst,' said the major. I could hardly believe what I was hearing; I was thrilled. 'Would you be interested?' he asked.

'Yes, sir,' I replied.

'Okay, march out.'

'Well done, son, keep it up,' said the sergeant-major, winking.

I felt about ten feet tall – me, an officer.

I couldn't wait to go and tell my mates; they were all pleased for me. I worked even harder than before, I was really going for it. The boat patrol I was to be taking part in was cancelled for a week, the actual day it went out was my nineteenth birthday, so the sergeant ordered me to go and get pissed. That night, Craig and I staggered into camp, full of Caribbean rum, we noticed that something was going on; the place was very busy, there was a helicopter flying back and forward, which was very unusual at weekends. I went into the ops room to see if Kev, a fellow signaller, had any idea what was happening.

'There has been a fucking boat crash,' he told me.

'You're fucking joking,' I said.

'One civvy dead and one of our guys lost half his leg.' I felt the hairs go up on the back of my neck. I was shocked.

Two rigid raiders (high-powered boats used by the army for river patrols) had been travelling towards each other and, for some reason, they had collided. One of the boats had lifted out of the water and crossed the path of the other, then the propeller had done all the damage.

The following week I was ordered to take part in a foot patrol, my job was as the patrol signaller and the medic. I would be working with four squaddies from my old platoon, which was good news as I knew we would have a good laugh. The night before we were due to depart, I signed out a radio and checked all my call signs. At the briefing we were told the patrol would last five days, we were to reconnoitre an old jungle track and check out a couple of old helicopter landing sites and if the landing sites were overgrown, we would set about clearing them as much as possible. We would have a soldier from the BDF (Belizean Defence Force) with us to act as a guide.

morning we sat at the helipad waiting and, as usual, the
er was late so we had a good moan. We reckoned the
would still be in the block, checking the gel in their hair
ana making sure they looked pretty. They were good at that.
After two hours the plan changed: we would drive there. We
moaned again as instead of a 30-minute flight we had a four-
hour drive, which would be quite boring.

We arrived in the small village of Aguacate an hour before
last light. There the village chief gave us a small hut to sleep in.
We made a scoff straightaway and then cleaned our weapons
down as they were covered in shit from the dusty roads. The
commander built a small fire and we all sat drinking tea and
bullshitting each other. Our guide, Cloyd, was having a moan
about the jungle.

'How many patrols have you done, Cloyd?' asked the
commander.

'This is my first,' he replied. I nearly swallowed my mug. This
guy had been in the Belizean Army for six years and had never
set foot in the jungle. 'I'm a chef,' he said.

We looked at each other, thinking the same thing. Something
like: 'Oh, fuck!' It was going to be a hard march through the
jungle and this guy was well overweight. We couldn't carry any
excess baggage because everyone would have to work really hard
as it was, the last thing we needed was some fat egg-frier to slow
us down. Our view was that the quicker we completed the
patrol task, the more time we could spend sunbathing or
swimming in the rivers.

Next morning the commander told us we could wear shorts
and T-shirts if we wanted to. This was good news as it would be
a lot cooler for us. A couple of blokes even made bandanas and
so we looked more like a bunch of renegades than members of
the British Army.

We thanked the village chief and then set off into the jungle.
It was only early morning but the heat was sweltering and I

could hardly walk with the weight of my kit, every step was hard work.

'Take five,' said the commander. I dropped to the ground. We had only covered about 400 metres but already I was soaked through with sweat. I lay there, enjoying the rest.

All too soon it was time to move. We plodded on up the small, muddy track, then after about five minutes the terrain changed and it became fairly rocky and small pools of water blocked the path and, at times, we had to cut through the trees. The ground started to rise quite steeply, too fucking steeply for my liking.

The patrol was spread out over a couple of hundred metres, with me at the back trying to help Cloyd, who was practically crawling.

'Stop here lads and get a drink.' We all sat together sipping water, no one spoke as we were all finding this a ball-breaker. 'Everybody feel all right?' asked the commander.

'Aye, never fucking better,' replied Rick.

The commander pulled out his map and showed us our intended route for the day. He reckoned we'd be very pushed to meet the chopper in four days' time if we carried on at this speed. We set off once again, still moving slowly and stopping every couple of minutes and taking every opportunity to rest our legs.

The hill got steeper and steeper until, at one point, we were on our hands and knees, scrambling over rocks. Less than an hour into the patrol and we were in a shit state. I thought that there must be easier ways to make a living than this torture. At least we all stopped on a short ledge to wait for the last stragglers. After a short while, Rick came staggering in saying: 'I'm fucked, I want to go home.' Then, eventually, Cloyd trundled in.

'You better move your fucking arse, you lazy bastard,' shouted the boss.

'My knee is sore, I can hardly walk,' Cloyd said to no one in particular. I took out the first-aid pack and gave Cloyd two painkillers. I had a look at his knee but it looked pretty normal with no swelling or anything. I think the sore knee was an excuse as the poor bastard was really struggling. I had a word with the commander and suggested we take things nice and slow, stopping every while for a break and some water as the heat was unbelievable and every piece of our clothing was soaking. We all looked as if we'd been in the jungle for days rather than hours. One at a time we set off up the hill, me and the commander at the rear to keep Cloyd company and give him some encouragement.

We had walked on for about 50 metres when I noticed how white Cloyd looked. 'We need to stop, Tony, and sort him out,' I said to the commander.

I gave Cloyd lots of water and a couple of dextrose tablets, then I stripped him to the waist and told him to lie in the shade. I was starting to get fucking worried as Cloyd didn't look too good at all.

'He can't carry any kit, we'll split it among us,' I said. I handed out his weapon, rucksack and his webbing between the lads.

'We need to get off this hill and get a camp set up,' Tony said.

'What about Cloyd?' I asked.

'We need to move him, even if we have to carry him.'

We all stood up, Cloyd didn't move at all. 'Fuck this! We need a helicopter,' I said. I opened my rucksack and set up my radio and I dialled in the correct frequency: 'Hello, hotel two zero, this is hotel one alpha, over.'

'Two one alpha, go ahead,' said the voice back at base.

'We are 3.5 kilometres from Aguacate and one member of the patrol has suspected heat exhaustion. We require helicopter evacuation, over,' I said, starting to flap.

'Wait one.'

Cloyd was marble white and still lying in the same position. We all sat in silence, waiting for the reply message from headquarters.

'Get some water down his neck and, for fuck's sake, someone talk to him!' I shouted. I was really fucking flapping.

'Two one alpha, you have to carry on with the patrol task, over,' came the message from HQ.

'Roger, out,' I said, hardly believing what they had said.

I packed the radio away and checked to make sure Cloyd was all right. He had stopped sweating and looked really bad. Now we were all in a state of panic and shock. We had been trained to deal with situations like this, but it had all happened so quickly.

The commander spread his map on the muddy ground. 'If we can move him to this, we can set up a basha [camp],' he said, pointing to a flat piece of ground on the map. Two of the guys picked up Cloyd and supported him on either side, while I grabbed his rifle and followed on behind. I can remember thinking back to my medic course and trying to remember how the fuck to treat someone with heat exhaustion? Then it came back to me: plenty of fluids, keep them cool and place a drip on them. I stopped, took off my rucksack and checked the first-aid kit and, sure enough, there was no fucking drip. Inwardly I cursed the useless cunts who made up these medical packs. As I repacked my rucksack, I could remember my instructor telling me heat exhaustion, if not treated properly, can quickly lead to death.

At the top of the hill Cloyd collapsed completely. I raced over and checked his breathing and his pulse. I put him in the recovery position. I said: 'Rick, keep your eye on him while I set the radio up.' I was fucking shitting myself – I think we all were. We were in the middle of nowhere, one guy down, no fucking drip and HQ thinking we are having a fucking ball.

'Hotel two zero, this is one alpha. Require urgent helicopter casevac [casualty evacuation], repeat, require urgent helicopter casevac over!' I shouted.

'Wait out.'

We waited and waited. We reckoned the controller would be sitting in the ops room, picking his fat lazy arse. Useless bastards! Twenty minutes passed before the word came back: the word was 'carry on'. 'Carry fucking on? I'll kill the bastards,' said the commander.

I remember thinking, 'Fuck this for a game of soldiers, I want to go home. Now, please.'

I went over and checked Cloyd was all right and, as I sat beside him, I realised we had to do something. This guy's life was in our hands.

'Rick and Johnny, start cutting a winch hole in the trees,' I said.

I grabbed the handset and started shouting over the radio. I explained the situation to the operations officer over the radio, his reply was 'okay'.

'No, it's not fucking okay!' I was shouting. The commander grabbed the radio handset and said he was demanding a helicopter now. The officer asked if he knew who he was speaking to. Then, just when you think things can't get any worse, they do.

'He has stopped breathing!' shouted Rick. I ran over to Cloyd and checked his airway to make sure it was clear; he bit down hard on my fingers and his jaw locked shut. Rick opened his mouth and I retrieved my digits intact. At that point my training took over, it was as if I was on autopilot. I started mouth-to-mouth resuscitation and I checked the pulse. No pulse. Oh, fuck! I was scared. 'Someone start cardiac compression, hurry up!' The commander changed places with me and I got straight on the radio. 'Two zero, this is two one alpha. I require a fucking medevac straightaway, the casualty has now stopped breathing, over!' I shouted.

'Roger, wait, out.'

'Two one alpha, helicopter will be with you shortly. Send grid reference, over,' said the base.

'Wait.' The commander decided that the helicopter would have difficulty finding us, he checked his map, there was a landing site about two miles away. We could meet it there and then fly back. I informed HQ about our intentions and I was told it would take 50 minutes for the helicopter to reach us. I had a decision to make then, something I would have to live with forever.

I was the only one with advanced medical training and I was also the only qualified signaller with the skills to talk the helicopter in. I couldn't do both jobs at once. Did I stay with Cloyd and hope the helicopter found us, or should I run to the landing site and talk the helicopter down? I decided Cloyd's condition was far too serious for my medical skills and our only hope was to get the helicopter here quickly, then he could be airlifted to hospital. 'Rick, when the helicopter comes over, fire a red one of these,' I said, handing him a flare gun. I grabbed a smoke grenade and the radio and left everything else as the less kit we had the faster we could cover the ground. The commander and I started running up the track, we both ran like fuck. The track was in a shit state and I tripped over a few times and got straight back up covered in mud and water. We both knew every minute was crucial; Cloyd's life depended on us. That really scared me, but it also made me run like a fucking madman.

I can't remember how long it took us to get there, but I do remember us jumping up and down with joy when we found the landing site. I set the radio up and checked my frequency then I held the smoke grenade and waited and waited.

'He is dead, man,' said a voice. I turned around and a small Mayan Indian had appeared, quite literally from nowhere. 'He is dead,' he kept repeating. I was starting to get really pissed off with this guy. My first thought was that how the fuck does he know that Cloyd is dead? It was strange, here we were in the jungle, no one for miles, or so we thought, and this guy just appeared from nowhere. It never occurred to me that he could have met the others further back up the track. My brain just couldn't make the connection at all. I was really confused.

The radio crackled into life: 'Two one alpha, this is rescue helicopter, viper two two, we'll be with you in five minutes.' I replied with a ten-figure grid reference and an update on the casualty. We could hear the helicopter in the distance and as the chopper got closer I started to talk him towards us, then, at the last minute, I set off the red smoke grenade, which nearly choked us. 'Roger two one alpha, I have your smoke visual.' The helicopter flew over the top of us and landed behind a huge wall of bushes. 'Fucking wanker,' said the commander. We both started running through the bushes, cutting ourselves to shreds. As we got nearer, the helicopter took off again but it had dropped the loadmaster who was running towards us with a drip in his hands. 'A bit fucking late for that,' I thought!

'We need the fucking chopper, get it back down!' shouted Tony. The loadie mumbled into the radio.

'The guy is nearly dead, you better fucking hurry up,' I said testily.

Thirty seconds later we jumped inside the helicopter. The unit medical officer was sitting beside the door and Tony showed the pilot where to go on the map. We flew fast and low over the jungle canopy and after about two minutes the helicopter went into a hover so I knew we were directly above Cloyd and the lads. I sat there unable to do anything, my part was over, all I could do was pray that everything would be all right.

I watched as the medical officer was winched down through the trees while we stayed in the hover for what seemed like ages, unaware what was going on below us. The loadmaster shouted that we were low on fuel and we would have to return to camp.

We flew straight back to the helipad at Rideau camp, where we had found a small welcoming party, which consisted of the commanding officer and other various hangers-on. While the helicopter refuelled, we briefed the CO on what had happened.

The helicopter lifted away, fast and low and I stood watching it, wondering if Cloyd was still alive. I was in deep shock and was still trying to take in what was going on. I had to sit down as I was feeling weak and tired now the adrenalin had stopped flowing. One of the officers told us to go and get cleaned up.

'No, sir, we'll wait till the helicopter comes back,' said Tony.

'I'll send someone up to let you know the score,' replied the officer nonchalantly.

Know the score?. This cunt thinks he is talking about some fucking football match or something as unimportant. So we did what we always did, we sat and we waited.

After 40 minutes, the chopper came screaming on to the helipad. I thought that everything was going to be all right as the helicopter was obviously in a hurry to get Cloyd to the hospital. I had more or less convinced myself that he was still alive. As the heli touched down I ran forward to the door. Cloyd was lying dead, wrapped in a green poncho, he wasn't brown anymore, he was blue. I stood and stared. I didn't know what to do or say. I turned and walked away from the helicopter, my mind just couldn't comprehend any of this madness. As I walked up the path the commanding officer stopped me. 'What do you think, Donnan?'

I didn't have a fucking clue what he was talking about. I was in no mood for any stupid games.

'I don't think anything, sir,' I replied.

'It was his fault, he was fat, should have kept himself fit, you know,' he was saying.

'Yes, sir,' I said. Any respect I had for the CO died there and then. I walked up to my room and had a wash, then changed my uniform. I sat on my bed, confused, angry and pissed off.

'Barry, make your way down to the guardroom, mate,' said Tony.

'What's going on?' I asked.

'Not a fucking clue,' he replied.

No one ever seemed to know what was going on, that's just the way the army is. We just fucked about from one thing to the next, in the hope that someone, somewhere, knew what was going on. At the guardroom I met the other members of the patrol. The local police had turned up and wanted individual statements from us. I was shown into a small room with two police officers.

'Name?' one of them asked.

'24823178, Fusilier Barry Donnan,' I said. I was then cautioned.

'Start from the beginning and tell us what happened,' said the police officer.

While I was explaining everything, the other one wrote everything down. Then he started asking me questions: Did anybody take drugs? Did anyone kick the shit out of Cloyd? Were we racist? 'We'll get to the bottom of this, we'll find out exactly what happened on that patrol.'

'Nothing happened,' I said, getting angry. I wanted to grab the policeman and shake him and tell him: 'Look, you've got it all wrong. Nothing happened, please listen, we tried all we could to save him. I know, I was there.' But I didn't. I don't know why.

'A post-mortem will be carried out in the morning, then we'll speak to you again,' he said, shuffling his papers.

I walked back to my room, feeling as if my world had shattered around me. Maybe I had made the wrong decision. Should I have stayed with him? What if the helicopter had been quicker? These thoughts were reeling through my mind and I didn't have the answers. The only thing I knew for sure was that someone had died, yeah, that bit was real.

I met up with the rest of the patrol in the NAAFI. We sat in a corner and tried to make sense of the past 24 hours. The commander told us not to panic, everything would be fine, we were in good hands, the British Army wouldn't let anything happen to us. I thought back to my first day in the army when our instructor told us we were all part of one big family and that the army always looked after its own. He fucking lied.

Next morning it was back to work as normal. I felt like shit. Rumours had already started doing the rounds. The first one I heard was that we beat up Cloyd because he was too slow and that things had just got out of hand. In the cookhouse, guys were walking past making comments like: 'Fuck going on patrol with you lot, we'd be coming back in a bodybag.' I was angry at these remarks but I never let it bother me, after all, what these clowns said didn't matter, it was the police we were worried about.

'What about the funeral?' I asked the commander.

'I'll find out this afternoon.'

I went back to my room and I sat alone trying hard to understand what the hell was going on. I tried hard to put things into some kind of order in my mind. I thought about Cloyd and the look on his face as he lay dead inside the helicopter. I couldn't believe he was gone. No more Cloyd Gillet. Dead, finished – it was so final.

The commander came to see me late afternoon. 'Bad news, the sergeant-major won't let us go to the funeral.'

'Why fucking not?' I asked.

'I don't fucking know, he wouldn't tell me,' said Tony. That really fucked me off. We battled to save the guy's life and we couldn't even pay our last respects without the army interfering. Tony carried on: 'And Special Investigation Branch are flying out from the UK this afternoon.'

'You're joking,' I said.

'No, I'm fucking not and – wait to you hear this – they want us back out on patrol within the next two days,' he said, smirking.

'Are you taking the piss?'

'No.'

Tony sat on the edge of my bed, with his head in his hands. I couldn't help feeling he was holding something back from us, something that us lowlifes didn't need to know.

Next morning the police came back as they wanted to speak to us again. I was informed that I was being interviewed under the suspicion of murder. I was scared, no one seemed to believe us and not one of the regiment's hierarchy came to see us. It was as if they didn't want to know what happened, they had already judged for themselves. I decided that I didn't want to play at soldiers anymore.

After our interviews we sat in the NAAFI drinking tea. We all came to the conclusion that we had to attend Cloyd's burial. It was our duty to be there and we all wanted to show respect and try and set the record straight. The commander went back to see the company sergeant-major, he explained how we felt, again he said no and told the commander to stop bothering him.

'What about the padre?' I suggested. We had an excellent padre, so we asked for his help.

'Leave it with me, lads,' he said. Within an hour the padre came to see us. He had sorted things out for us. Good old padre. He sat with us for a while and asked how we felt. He told us not to worry, that God would look after us. I thought that I wish He would fucking hurry up.

After dinner we went to the NAAFI with one aim in mind: to get pissed out of our minds and have a fucking good moan. If life is shit, you're about to be charged with murder and no one cares, go and get drunk and smash up your room, that was our attitude.

Later on, I went to the toilets and cried, at least no one could see me in there. Soldiers don't cry, do they? I realised that we were all victims in this farce, just as Cloyd was, the only difference was that he was dead and we were still alive. It seemed as if everyone had let us down, including the British Army. I had become quite disillusioned with my beloved regiment. They had ignored us when we needed them most. Things had changed in the space of a week.

Next day it was the turn of the Special Investigation Branch (STB) to interview us. A post-mortem had been carried out on Cloyd and his death was attributed to asphyxia. I didn't really know what that was so I asked the officer to explain.

'Lack of oxygen in the body, caused by the interruption of breathing,' he said dryly.

'Oh,' I said, thinking that didn't sound too good.

'Take a look at these,' he said, throwing me a handful of black-and-white photographs. I started looking through them; they were pictures of Cloyd's body after the post-mortem. I started to shake. 'Not very nice, eh?' he said. I couldn't answer him. 'Where did all the bruises come from, his body was covered with them?' he asked.

'That must be from the heart massage and . . .' I said.

'Fucking rubbish,' he said, cutting me off. 'You lot did that. You gave the guy a kicking, didn't you? Things just got out of hand a bit.'

'No, we fucking didn't,' I replied.

'Well, explain these bruises,' he said, holding the photos up to my face.

'I don't know where they came from.'

'Look at it from our point of view. Four British soldiers out on patrol with a black soldier and less than 24 hours into the patrol and he's dead,' he was saying. 'How do you think his wife and family feel? He only had six weeks left in the army, then he was going to live in America,' he said, spitting all over me.

'Funny that,' I thought, 'I'm finding out more about Cloyd now he is dead, more than I would have known had he still been alive.'

The interview carried on for about an hour. Well, it wasn't

really an interview, I sat there and listened while he dictated to me. He explained to me that this incident was so serious that Downing Street had been informed. I think maybe he was bull-shitting me. He also added that this was just the beginning and that things would get worse before they got better. Just what I needed to hear, that really made my day that did.

I went back to my room and changed into my running kit. I wanted to go for a long run and get some anger and pain out of my system. At the front gate I was stopped by the sentry. 'You're not allowed to leave the camp,' he said.

'Said who?' I asked.

'The guard commander – I'm sorry, mate.'

I couldn't believe it, they actually thought we might go AWOL, perhaps fuck off to Mexico or somewhere. Come to think of it, that would have been a good idea, but that would only make them more suspicious. They were treating us like small boys and it pissed me off.

Later that afternoon I was questioned by the SIB again, only this time there were two of them. They asked the same questions and I gave them the same answers. They reckoned they had enough evidence to charge us, but they just didn't know who was being charged with what. Inside I was angry. I was like a walking time-bomb. I wanted to shout, 'Fucking enough, the joke is fucking over, leave us alone, we're innocent, aren't we?' I was beginning to question myself and the others. Maybe we did do something untoward. I went and sat alone and replayed everything in my mind just to make sure. Was any of this real? It was my fault, I should have stayed with Cloyd right to the end. I felt guilty. Why me? Why Cloyd? Why any of us? I didn't know anything, I was deeply confused, yet again. Someone, somewhere, knew how the army was treating us and that disgusted me. Life was pretty shit, at least I thought so, it was time for some good old alcohol to help dull the senses. I met the other patrol members in the bar. We drank silly amounts of booze and we said stupid things to each other. We still believed that we could put things right at the funeral. This was more wishful thinking on our part.

We met outside the guardroom at 0900 hours, dressed in full combats. Our padre was coming to the funeral with us to give us some moral support. We needed it.

We drove the short distance to the church in Belize City, here we would meet the cortège. We stood in a small group outside and we were shitting ourselves. Four Royal Military Police turned up, apparently for our protection. 'Why, what's going to happen?' asked our commander.

'Just a precaution,' was the reply.

The military cop explained that this was the third mysterious death of a BDF soldier at the hands of the British Army and we could be subjected to some form of reprisal. The BDF soldiers put this down as another racist killing and they were refusing to go out on patrol with the British Army. 'Now they fucking tell us,' I thought.

One BDF soldier had been killed with his own rifle. It was a tragic accident. One of the British soldiers asked to see this guy's weapon as they carried better rifles than we did, but he didn't know it was loaded and there was a round up the spout as this was not normal British practice. So the soldier had a play around with the rifle then, jokingly, he aimed at the BDF guy and pulled the trigger. He blew the guy's head off. We didn't know much about the other incident – other than it too happened deep in the jungle – and now there was Cloyd's death. They all wanted someone to blame, a scapegoat if you like, and it looked like that was our role.

We stopped talking when we saw the cortège. I had never seen anything like it in my life. At the front was a jazz band playing 'When The Saints Come Marching In', while at the back the mourners were dancing and singing. They were wearing bright clothes and some of them were even wearing sunglasses. Behind the coffin were hundreds of people, including about 50 from the BDF. I was numb, I was also very scared.

As the family walked past they glared at us and Cloyd's brother shouted that we were murdering bastards. A couple of BDF soldiers tried to spit on us and said they were going to kill us. I knew, given the chance, they would not think twice about it. The look of hatred on their faces said it all.

We were last inside the church and we sat right at the back. They were all staring at us. I sat with my head bowed as I didn't want to antagonise anyone. I actually feared for my life at that point. I wanted to get out of the church and run somewhere, anywhere, away from this fucking madness.

As Cloyd's coffin was wheeled into the church the place went mad. People started shouting and screaming and the atmosphere was very tense. The coffin was opened. Cloyd was dressed in a black shroud and several people went over and took a picture. He looked so different, bloated and white, it didn't look like the Cloyd we knew. As I write these words today, I can still recall the face of Cloyd, the face that would haunt me, the face that would slip into my mind and my dreams. It still scares me when I think about it.

The service was very short. We sang a couple of songs and listened to Cloyd's commanding officer as he spoke about him. I don't remember what was said, I tried to conjure up some reason for this but my mind had ceased to function. I was numb, I couldn't take anything else in. The minister summed up by saying that yet again this was a suspicious death at the hands of the British Army and that something must be done about it. We shifted uneasily in our seats. It felt like the whole church had their eyes on us. I thought they were going to lynch us there and then, or would they wait until we were outside?

We marched behind the coffin, all the way through the filthy streets of Belize. We stayed beside our brigadier. There was a good reason for this as we figured that no one would harm us if we were standing beside the highest-ranking officer in Belize.

We kept to the back of the crowds at the graveside. As the coffin was lowered down, Cloyd's wife and children were screaming. I wanted to tell them the whole story, that we didn't kill him and that his death had been quick and peaceful. Surely that's what Cloyd would have wanted? But we didn't, because we were too scared. I had no wish to die.

Before the service finished, we sneaked away and on to the truck to go back to the safety of the camp. We changed into shorts and headed to the bar and we drank far too much for our own good. But what else was there? This was all we knew, the only escape we had was booze.

I decided that day that my army career was over, I would get out as soon as we got back to England. I couldn't believe how we had been treated over the last few days, it really fucking disgusted me. I had no wish to be part of this madness, I was tired and let down. I learned something that day. I learned that Cloyd and us, in fact, all soldiers, are expendable, we are all cannon fodder and no one gives a fuck about us, least of all the army. We were nothing more than a name and number, Queen and country and all that bullshit. 'Fuck this,' I thought, 'I'll leave while I'm still breathing.' Why did Cloyd have to go and fucking die on patrol with us? He didn't have to suffer any more. The only person who could help us was lying in a graveyard outside Belize City. I began to feel really guilty. What if I had stayed with Cloyd instead of running to meet the helicopter, would he still be alive? I felt I had made the wrong decision, it was my fault. Someone was dead, all because of me. It troubled me deeply, it consumed everything.

Next day we were again interviewed by the SIB. They said it was just to check over the statements. That was more lies. They asked me to go over everything again, which I did. That was easy because I had already been over it a thousand times in my mind.

'Why wasn't there a drip in the medical pack?' one of them asked.

'You tell me, you know everything else,' I said.

They didn't like that. 'Don't get fucking smart, sonny,' said the sergeant-major. 'I'll ask you again, why wasn't there a drip in the med pack?'

'I don't fucking know, I'm just a nobody, go and ask the medical officer,' I replied.

'Listen, mate, you're up to your neck in shit, you need us,' he was saying.

'Yeah, yeah,' I thought. I stopped listening and stared at the fan whirling away in the corner. I wasn't playing this game any more. He was telling lies again.

'You realise this will go to court?'

'Yes, sir,' I replied nonchalantly. I didn't care anymore, what was the point? I had no control over anything that was going on, so why worry? Fuck them all, they could do what they wanted. I felt like a pawn in a chess game, except that we could only move backwards.

That night I was back on stag in the ops room and I enjoyed the peace and quiet. No dead soldiers in there, no nothing, just plenty of radios. I wished I had never insisted on doing a jungle patrol. Life was so easy in the ops room. Easy and safe.

After my shift was finished, I headed to the block for a shower and a kip. It wasn't going to happen. 'Donnan, you've got to go and see the SIB,' said the company runner. I changed into fresh combats and walked to headquarters. Outside the building I met the SIB officer.

'Are you looking for me, sir?' I asked.

'No, it's all right, I'll speak to you when you get back,' he said.

'Back from where, sir?'

'Your regiment is sending you back to the jungle.'

I thought this was another joke, but no, sure enough, we were sent back to the jungle for five days, this time with two

BDF soldiers instead of one. How thoughtful of them.

The army actually wanted us to go back on the route where Cloyd had died; fortunately they had the sense to change their minds at the last minute. We spent five days in the jungle doing nothing. It was great, we lay about in the sun and relaxed. There was a river nearby, so we would go down there and have a swim. At night we would light a small fire and sit around it drinking tea. The conversation was always the same: life outside the army. Most of us had decided it was time to leave and move on to new things. Enough was enough, what with Lockerbie and now this incident with Cloyd. I was 19 and beginning to feel like an old man, nothing could be as bad as this.

I could have stayed in the jungle forever, I loved it, it was good to be away from the camp and all the bullshit we had left behind. Our BDF soldiers never mixed with us at all and I suppose you couldn't blame them.

On the morning of our pick-up, we packed our kit and headed to the landing site, which was about 50 metres away. The helicopter was late, as usual. So we sat and waited, as usual. Seventy minutes later the helicopter landed and out jumped a photographer.

'Right, lads, I'm going to take pictures of you boarding the Puma,' said the cameraman.

'Why?' asked the commander.

'I'm writing a book about the British Army.'

'Would you like a picture of my arse?' the commander asked.

We all laughed. It wasn't very funny, but we all felt it was an appropriate gesture to the British Army. The photographer must have thought we were a strange bunch. Our ugly mugs later appeared in the book *The British Army in Colour*, that was our claim to fame.

Back at camp things were pretty normal, normal for everyone else that is. We learned that Cloyd's family wanted his body exhumed for a second post-mortem; the first one had been

by a white army doctor and they felt he could have
. Why couldn't they leave Cloyd alone? It was just
tion that no one could answer.

The SIB had passed the case to the Belizean authorities, who
would hold a coroner's inquest in a few weeks' time to decide the
outcome. There was more bad news: I was going on a NCO's
cadre, this would be my first step for promotion to lance-corporal,
or lance-comical as we called them. I didn't have the interest
anymore, my heart wasn't in it. I had seen too many guys do the
course and become Hitlers overnight, plus I had enough on my
plate with the inquest coming up. I went to see the company
commander and explained the situation. He said it was not
debatable, he also reminded me that I was paid to follow orders,
not to question them. 'Cheers, sir,' I thought, 'nothing like an
understanding boss, remind me to do the same for you one day!'

The army was so blind it never even realised how fucked up
we all were, I was sick of it. I began to resent authority and
everything it stood for, the system had let us down too many
times. More than anything I wanted to go home, back to my
mum, back where things made sense.

Sometimes at night, when we were feeling down, we would
sneak over to the pool and shit in it, or put big ugly toads in the
water. After we got bored with that we turned our attention to
the washing-lines of the officers' mess. A couple of us would
creep in, one would keep a lookout while the other set about
cutting the clothes in half. This was our stupid way of getting
back at the retarded wankers. It made us feel better, anyway.

One night, on such an escapade, Craig and I thought we were
going to be eaten alive by some exotic jungle beast. We had
crawled through barbed wire and up a small stream into the
laundry hut, hoping to acquire para smocks, which were far
superior to our jackets. The hut was basically a leafy roof supported by several logs. Once inside, we carefully examined
everything, but we couldn't use torchlight as the area was

patrolled by guards. All of a sudden I heard splashing and grunting, it was coming up the stream towards us. The grunting got louder. Oh fuck, it sounded like a wild boar. We'd heard stories of them eating people. 'Quick, up here,' Craig said, almost inside the roof.

'Fucking place will be crawling with tarantulas,' I exclaimed.

As the beast got nearer I thought that maybe the roof wasn't such a bad idea, so I scrambled up to the rafters. We could hear it sniffing and walking about below us but it was so dark we couldn't see anything. 'We're fucked!' Craig said.

Suddenly the 'thing' came into sight below us. It was a golden Labrador. I couldn't believe it, where it came from I don't know. I laughed so much I fell to the ground. It cheered me up so much, I hadn't had a laugh in ages. Come to think of it we didn't have much to laugh about.

At night-time I started having strange dreams, all I remember is sitting in a tree with Cloyd, while below were people I knew, yes, they were my family. They were standing around a grave. My grave. Other times I was back at Lockerbie, lying beside the bodies in the cockpit, unable to move. The dreams were so vivid and so frightening that some nights I woke up screaming. I never told anyone about them, I thought naively it would pass, time being a great healer and all that stuff.

On duty I would tune in to the BBC World Service, just to relieve the boredom. One night, I remember slouching on my desk when I heard the news that someone had invaded Kuwait. I sat up and listened in, trying hard to remember where Kuwait was. I heard the Middle East mentioned, but thought it was too fucking far away for us to worry about. I switched off the radio.

Next morning it was all the gossip that somewhere had been invaded. Nobody was really that interested; if it didn't affect us there and then, it wasn't worth worrying about. Our sergeant reckoned otherwise. 'If they send out British troops we may have to stay out here longer,' he said, looking serious. He was a clever man, so I believed him, as he knew things we didn't.

That was all we needed, another tour of this place. Trust somebody to go and start a fucking war, when all I wanted was home and out of the army. Just when you think things can't get any worse, they always do. Something about frying pans and fires came to mind.

The following week I reported to Holdfast camp in northern Belize for my NCO's cadre, there were about 30 of us. The chief instructor greeted us: 'Gentlemen, for the next three weeks your arse is mine. When I say jump, you ask how high? When I say run, you ask how far? Do you fucking understand?' shouted the boss.

'Yes, sir,' we all shouted.

'Do you fucking understand?' he asked again.

'Yes, sir!' we shouted again, a bit louder.

'How fucking original,' I thought. These instructors always said the same things, they must learn these stupid phrases on some special course. It was almost as though they had their own language.

'Back out here in 20 minutes, dressed in PT kit,' he ordered.

We dashed inside and got changed straightaway as we knew they wouldn't give us the full 20 minutes. Sure enough, after about four minutes came the order to get on parade. The instructor told us that we were too slow and that he would have to teach us a lesson. He took us on a run that I'll never forget, it was a killer. After that we had a room inspection. The boss came in with white gloves on looking for dust, he found some under a bed. 'Outside, now!' came the order. This time we had to race round the camp with a five-gallon jerrycan full of water. I was fucked and this was only the first day. That night was spent scrubbing the rooms till three in the morning, then it was back up at five for battle PT. That sounded glamorous, but it was nothing more than a long, fast run carrying a telegraph pole. What a nice way to start off the day.

After breakfast it was time for various lectures, mainly about army law and how to teach people. Someone always nodded off, so it would be back outside for some more physical punishment.

The course was all about pressure, with lots of shouting and racing about and everything to be done in double time. However hard we worked, it was never good enough for the instructors, so we spent more time doing punishment PT than anything else. I had never worked so hard since leaving the training depot two years before.

Night-time would be spent swotting up on weapons and tactics, as there is more to being an infantry soldier than just running around dressed in combats – well, sometimes.

On my fourth morning I was ordered to change into fresh combats and pack an overnight bag. Cloyd's inquest was being held today in Belize City, but someone had forgotten to tell me. When I arrived at the magistrates' court, the proceedings had already started. The courtroom was packed with Cloyd's family and soldiers from the BDF. My regiment had sent a platoon commander for moral support.

The proceedings stopped for a short break and the chief magistrate was sacked as the authorities decided he was too racist for such a sensitive case. All that day we listened very carefully to the statements given by doctors, police and Cloyd's commanding officer. We learned some interesting things, all points that were relevant to the investigation, but someone, somewhere, decided we hadn't needed to know – after all, we were only the grunts, we didn't matter. It turned out that Cloyd had failed his last army medical, also that he had never set foot in the jungle in his army career as he was a chef. The BDF had sent him on patrol so they could keep their expert soldiers for an exercise that weekend and they had known the state he was in before they sent him out. It had cost him his life.

As I sat and listened to these revelations, I was shocked. It filled me with absolute despair and left me feeling vulnerable. I ımed to play my small part in this sorry state of affairs. ᵣmed my thoughts that as far as soldiers go we are all ıble. I tried to convince myself that it was for something, but it wasn't, none of this should have happened, it was all for nothing. Just like a big game. That made me sad. The real killers were the ones who decided to send Cloyd out on patrol, the very ones who were trying to blame us. The court was full of liars and hypocrites and we were not impressed.

On the third day the jury retired for 30 minutes to prepare its verdict. We sat and played the waiting game – once again! On the jury's return, the foreperson said that the deceased was in a deteriorating state of health and was also overweight. His death was from asphyxia and no one could be held criminally res-ponsible. I was happy with the outcome, but there were no win-ners in this game, we had all lost something. I blacked out after that and next thing I remember was being in the military hospital recovering.

Next morning, after breakfast, I was handed a copy of *Amandala*, which is the local newspaper in Belize City, we had made the front page. The headline was INQUEST CLEARS FUSILIERS IN BDF DEATH. It was a basic article covering the in-quest and it confirmed my fears that many people still believed we were guilty of murder. Under a headline titled FAIR IS FOUL, AND FOUL IS FAIR was a lengthy article about Cloyd's death. It said:

> A BDF soldier is dead. He died under mysterious circumstances. His death arouses suspicion in the minds of his fellow Belizean soldiers. They want to make sure that their worst fears are not true. They want a fair and thorough inquiry into the matter. The matter is not as straightforward as it appears. The BDF soldier is a black Belizean, he is on patrol, alone, with four white British soldiers. This is the first mistake the system had made. Don't send out one Belizean with

several British soldiers. It is not fair to either group. So here is this patrol, one BDF, four British, going through the jungle on 21 July. According to the British soldiers, the BDF Private, Cloyd Gillet, starts complaining of pain in his left knee. They rested for about five minutes. They then continued on patrol. The BDF soldier again complains, especially as they began ascending a hill. The situation with the BDF soldier gets so bad that his British colleagues say that they relieved him of his load – his backpack and webbing. While descending a hill the BDF soldier falls. He rolls towards a tree, where he hitches up. He appears to be in bad shape. He is given first aid, mouth-to-mouth attempts at resuscitation, pressure is put on his chest, several pumps are given to the back region to revive his heart. There is no pulse, no breathing. A helicopter for which the soldiers had radioed arrives. Private Cloyd Gillet is put in a bag and winched up, strapped under his arms. This, the British soldiers say, accounts for the deep bruise marks on his shoulders. There were three Mayans in the area. They may or may not have seen what happened. Their statements to the police are read to them in court. What little they see is of no value in shedding any light on what really occurred. A coroner's inquest is held into the death of Private Cloyd Gillet. The chief magistrate is the coroner. His court is crowded on all days of the hearing. The court is a study in contrasts. Several white British soldiers decked out in camouflage gear, neat and impressive, the guardians of our territorial sovereignty, several black Belizean soldiers dressed in green uniforms looking sombre. The jury sits out front at the table, they are young, very young and, incidentally, they are brown. As I peep into the court and survey this scene, I remember Zelma Jex's poem 'What Colour is a Man?'. At the table with the jurors sits a black man, a lawyer, he is there defending and protecting the interests of the white soldiers. There is no one in court defending the interests of the black

Belizean soldiers. Those who complain say that this is the third time a Belizean soldier had been on patrol with British soldiers and died under mysterious circumstances. They are the ones who must work with the British, they are the ones whose lives are on the line. They must know whether they are treated with respect and dignity they deserve. After all, not one, but three Belizean soldiers have died – all under mysterious circumstances. Is anything wrong? Let's discuss it, let's get it out in the open and if there is a problem let us try to solve it. We cannot have this type of tension in the army. But the coroner's inquest is flawed. It is a flawed link in a flawed chain. That chain is the system itself. The system let us down when it sent out one BDF man with four British soldiers (because there were already two mysterious deaths). The system let us down when it allowed one doctor to perform the post-mortem. The doctor told the inquest that the bruises on the body are not inconsistent with bruises that could have been caused from rolling down a hill. Is there such a thing as a second opinion?

The system had let them down, but what about us, surely it had let us down too? More importantly, hadn't it let Private Cloyd Gillet down? After all, he was the one lying in a coffin, 24 years old and dead. Maybe we were all to blame, each of us playing a part, however small, just like in a film. Everybody wanted answers, the military police wanted answers, the BDF wanted answers and so did I. Yet when we told the truth, no one believed us as it wasn't what they wanted to hear. They had all conjured up dramatic stories in their own minds. They wanted to hear that we had killed Cloyd because of racial hatred, but that simply wasn't true.

I sat on the edge of the bed, holding the newspaper with tears rolling down my face. Although I had a major part in this film, I realised that no matter how much I protested our innocence, some people would always look on us as killers.

'Get your kit together – you're going back to camp, Donnan,' said the doctor, pulling me from my dazed state.

'Yes, sir,' I replied, forgetting almost immediately what he had said. Twenty minutes later I was still sitting in the same position, staring into space.

'Come on, Donnan, move your arse, the transport is here to take you back,' said the NCO, popping his head round the door.

'Give me two minutes,' I said as I jumped from the bed and started packing my kit.

'Oh, and also a message came from your regiment – you've been kicked off your NCO's cadre.'

'Why?' I asked.

'I don't have a clue, mate.'

'Cheers, anyway,' I said, sarcastically.

That was all I needed, more fucking bad news, as if it would be anything else. Any chance I had for promotion had gone, all my hard work lost in an instant, Cloyd's death had screwed up my life.

It was early afternoon when I arrived back at the camp, I was tired and feeling low, everything seemed different somehow, as if I didn't belong in the army any more. Officers and people I had once held in high regard now irritated the shit out of me, I was disillusioned with the whole fucking lot. The only thing that kept me going was the fact that I'd be heading back home in three weeks. I couldn't wait to see my family again.

After lunch I met Tony walking back from the cookhouse. The sergeant-major had asked him to take our patrol 'off side for a bit and get them pissed'. This was their method of counselling us. We were all emotional cowards, too busy running around doing macho things, no time to worry about how screwed up our heads were becoming, that didn't matter, did it?

Two hours later we were on a speedboat heading out to the Cayes – groups of islands along the barrier reef. It was a

Caribbean paradise with palm trees and white sand. We had only one thing in mind and that was to get very drunk, to that end we had six cases of beer loaded on to the boat. As the boat docked, an American tourist who had been travelling with us fell overboard and we laughed. We always laughed at other people's misfortune as it showed we didn't care. The Yank had stupidly challenged us to a drinking competition on the way over, and it was as he stood up to be sick that he tripped and went into the water. We won and the prize was a scoff on the Yank's boat later on. The guy was fuming. We plonked ourselves down beside the pier and got pissed, only moving to go to the toilet. None of us felt much like exploring the island or mixing with the locals, we just wanted to escape all the madness of the previous weeks. We drank and drank.

'Hi, guys!' It was the Yank again, he was pretty drunk.

'Fuck off!' said the commander.

'I've made some food for you guys.'

'Fuck off and die!' he was told.

'I've got some booze.'

We relented and staggered behind him as he showed us to his yacht. More booze was the last thing we needed. Our dinner consisted of spam and a handful of rice and it was disgusting, worse than army food. Our host then appeared with a bottle of whisky, which we helped empty. We all sat on the deck talking shit and winding up the American. It was a mistake.

'Right, you fuckers – I'm going to kill you all,' he said, waving a pistol in our direction. We started laughing, maybe it was nerves. 'You fucking soldiers are all the same.'

I started getting angry, in fact, I was raging. 'Go for it, arsehole, fucking shoot me,' I said, jumping to my feet.

He pointed the pistol straight at my head. 'Don't move,' he said.

All the time I was thinking, this is it, after everything we've been through, now some half-drunk American mouthpiece was going to kill us. For some reason I wasn't frightened, just annoyed it was going to end like this. Then I thought maybe he was a hitman, hired by Cloyd's family to get rid of us. I think I was being paranoid.

'Goodbye, motherfuckers,' he was saying as he pulled the trigger. Click! It was fucking empty, no rounds in the chamber. 'Just a wind up,' the Yank said and started laughing. I dived forward and kicked him hard in the bollocks and he went straight down.

'Fucking civvies,' said Rick, shaking his head. It seemed like I always attracted trouble.

Next day it was back to camp and the endless round of eating, sleeping and working in the ops room; it was hell. The army never mentioned Cloyd's death again, it was as if it had never happened, I sometimes thought I'd imagined the whole thing. Was it for real? Yeah, it was, the nightmares made sure I would never forget. Most mornings when I was having a wash, I couldn't even look at myself in the mirror as I felt guilty about Cloyd's death. Was it our fault? Today, as I write this book nearly eight years on, I still ask myself the same questions. I search my mind for answers but I don't have any. None of it made sense then and it sure as hell doesn't now, but I must keep trying. I owe it to myself. If I can't understand it, what chance does anyone else have?

Meanwhile, thousands of miles away in the Middle East, things were hotting up as Britain and many other countries were assembling troops in the Saudi desert. We definitely weren't going to the Gulf, our regimental officers had assured us of that. So that was good news.

The last few days in Belize were spent packing kit and dreaming, mainly about how we would spend our three weeks' disembarkation leave. The whole regiment was buzzing. Me, well, I just wanted home so that I could leave this so-called man's army, that was my only dream.

As the VC-10 thundered up the runway, I looked out of my small window, nothing much to see, lots of trees and shit. I was happy to be leaving Belize, alive! What had I learned in Belize? Several things: trust no one and that sometimes life can be cruel, and oh, something else – something more important – we were all just cannon fodder at the end of the day, as expendable as the very uniform we wore.

Poor Cloyd, I don't want to think about you, Cloyd. We all let you down, didn't we? I felt as if we had betrayed him, leaving him in that cold, dark and overcrowded graveyard in Belize City. One day I'll return there, I don't know why I want to go back, perhaps through respect or maybe it's in the hope that I can understand some little thing, like the last piece of a jigsaw, making everything complete.

We reached Oakington Barracks the following day. It was a mad rush as we handed in our kit and collected our travel warrants for the journey home. Sixty of us boarded the train for Glasgow and within an hour we were all pissed and, in true squaddie-style, we made complete arses of ourselves. Several guys were arrested at Newcastle for swinging on the train door when we were travelling at over a hundred miles an hour.

Back home things seemed different, things had changed. At the time I thought everyone in my family had become strange, now I realise it was me who had changed. I couldn't adjust back to family life. I knew my parents would never understand how fucked up I was after Lockerbie and Belize, so I never even tried to explain. At night I would lie awake for hours, too frightened to sleep as the nightmares were a bit vivid for my liking. Most nights I would end up cycling around the streets, or out walking – anything but sleeping. It was a lonely time. I felt as if I was on the moon. I had lost my sense of humour and I was like an old man. I just couldn't understand what was happening. I would always end up crying. Who for? Was it Cloyd? Or was it for me? Nothing mattered any more, what was the point of all this? I had an ace up my sleeve, though. If things got really bad, I would join Cloyd and his gang. I thought that being dead would be easier than all this torture.

5. You Could Knock Me Down with a Feather

We had gathered outside the company office in Oakington Barracks on our first day back at work after almost four weeks' leave. Everyone was well pissed off and the first day back is always hard work, trying to make the transition from civvy to being a robotic squaddie.

'Company, attention!' snarled the sergeant-major. He then started walking up and down the ranks, inspecting us for haircuts and shit like that. 'Donnan, am I hurting you?' he screamed in my ear.

'No, sir.'

'Well, I should be – I'm standing on your fucking hair! Get it fucking cut, you fucking tart!'

'Yes, sir,' I replied, wishing I could tell him to fuck off and get a life.

'Right, you fucking lot, leave is finished, no more lying about all day picking your holes – no more tea in fucking bed . . .' Someone behind me sniggered, none of us dared even move. 'Do you find something funny? Yes, you, CUNT!' screamed the sergeant-major, moustache twitching and the pace stick being waved around as if he was some kind of wizard.

'No, sir,' replied the voice behind me.

'Corporal James, get this fucking reptile out of my sight – now! Take him to the guardroom and throw away the key.' This was the shock treatment designed to make us switch on. I found the whole thing quite pathetic. Grown men running around screaming and shouting, trying to see who could be the nastiest. 'Sergeant Roberts, double the company round the hangars to waken them up,' ordered the sergeant-major.

'Yes, sir,' said Roberts, in his best arse-licking voice. 'By the front, double march!'

So, for the next 50 minutes we ran around hangars, did press-ups and snapped to attention 20 or 30 times. And why? Well, because the sergeant-major was in a bad mood and we needed it, or so he thought. How nice of him. The wanker!

We were all trained soldiers, professionals if you like, just like the army slogan: 'Be the Best'. No one mentioned that we would be treated like five-year-olds most of the time. As I pushed out yet another press-up on the cold, wet ground, I thought of the fat, lying colour sergeant in the army careers office the day I signed my life away. He told me about all the adventure training we would do, like climbing, windsurfing and sailing. He never mentioned the dead bodies and the amount of bullshit you could expect to encounter. I wonder why? I had been in the army almost three years and had never once been windsurfing or sailing. The careers office should have pictures of mutilated corpses just to make sure everyone who signs up knows exactly what they may have to deal with. Then maybe potential recruits would think long and hard about their glittering job in the army. In fact, the army recruiting office should be charged under the Job Descriptions Act. No one told me that I would be lifting dead bodies at Lockerbie and Belize, no one told me that we would be treated like dog shit. It was a very different life from the one portrayed by the recruiting sergeant that day I signed on as a young, naive 16-year-old boy. To make matters worse, he was a member of my regiment.

There is something about the Royal Highland Fusiliers and liars. The ability to tell a lie must be part of the promotion course for sergeants and above, it was something they were all good at. It seemed to me that the enemy were the senior non-commissioned officers within the regiment, they had no other purpose than to fuck everyone about. So much for the big family that would always look after us, what they really meant was that they would look after themselves.

The first week back in camp was spent cleaning things – everything that didn't move was scrubbed or polished till it was gleaming. There was a saying in the regiment at that time: 'Join the army and see the world – join the RHF and clean the world.'

Barrack-room soldiering, however, was a pretty safe option as there were no dead bodies to clean up, just plenty of empty beer cans – drinking was still the number one recreation for us grunts. The ability to drink like a fish did help make life a bit more bearable. I wasn't the only one finding life difficult. One night on guard duty, I found my partner with a loaded rifle in his mouth about the blow his brains all over the loading bay.

'What the fuck are you all about?' I stupidly asked.

'Fuck off, leave me alone,' he said.

'Look, mate, do you mind waiting and doing it somewhere else? I couldn't handle scraping bits of you off the fucking wall,' I said, frightened.

'Fuck you!'

Those extra few seconds made all the difference. He decided not to be so stupid, after all, it's only life and things couldn't really get any worse, could they? We walked into the guardroom and never mentioned a word to anyone, otherwise the poor fucker would have ended up in the jail if the guard commander had found out. As I lay down to sleep that night, I prayed that we would all get through this, after all in a few months I would be a civvy again, as long as the commanding officer agreed to release me early from my contract.

I recognised the smell before I opened my eyes, it was the heavy stench of death, that sweet, sickly smell that catches the back of your throat. I couldn't move, something was lying across my chest. All around me the aircraft lay broken. Where was I? It was dark, I wanted to shout and scream that I was still alive, but my mouth wouldn't open. My heart was pounding, why couldn't they see me? Please, help me someone. I was lying beside the wreckage of *Clipper Maid of the Seas* in a field near Tundergarth with dead bodies all around me. I was back in Lockerbie again, it was so real, I could see everything going on around me. 'Aaaarrrggghhh!' I sat upright, still screaming. Where the fuck was I?

'Shut the fuck up, you prick!' shouted someone beside the TV. 'We're trying to watch a fucking porno here.'

My heart felt as if it were about to jump out of my ribcage, my combats were soaked in sweat and it took me a couple of minutes to realise where I was. After that night I never slept in a bed again. I figured that if I didn't sleep in a bed, then I wouldn't have nightmares. Stupid or what? Some of my room-mates started calling me 'Mad'. Maybe I was. All I know is that things were getting to me. My head wasn't working properly any more, yet here was I on guard duty, protecting the whole camp, me and my faithful rifle, complete with 30 rounds of ammunition. The consequences if one of us flipped on duty didn't bear thinking about. Most of us needed protection from ourselves, never mind the enemy.

Unknown to me, I had started sliding down that slippery slope into mental illness, a journey that would take me to hell and back. The next few years would be the darkest period of my life. If I knew then what I know now, things would have been different. Why? Well, because I wouldn't be here today to write this book. I would have walked round the back of the guard-room and blown my brains out. I had spent my entire childhood wanting to be a soldier, and now, well, all I wanted was to be free and have a normal life, it's not much to ask, is it? But some-one had other ideas.

Saddam Hussein was causing serious problems in Kuwait and war looked pretty imminent when the United Nations had authorised the use of force if Iraq didn't withdraw before 15 January 1991. It seemed as if every other unit in the British Army was being deployed there, except us. This pissed a lot of blokes off as many felt this would be a good chance to put their training to the test, while others simply wanted a fight, a chance to kill someone for real. Squaddies love nothing more than a fucking good battle.

The regimental sergeant-major (RSM) called a scale-A parade one afternoon, which basically means everybody in the regiment must attend, even the cooks and attached personnel. We all gathered in the lecture theatre, anticipating what was going on but, in truth, no one had a fucking clue. 'Battalion, attention!' snarled the RSM. The whole regiment snapped to attention as one. It was quite impressive, none of us dared move. In came the commanding officer, as I said before there was a touch of Father Christmas about him. He was a big man, well, when I say big, what I really mean is fat – he looked as if he hadn't taken part in any physical training for a number of years.

'Gentlemen, we are here this afternoon to quash any rumours about our possible deployment to Saudi Arabia – it simply won't happen.' The CO went on to tell us that as a home defence unit we had no possible role in the Gulf, it was all down to the armoured regiments in Germany. In fact, he said: 'You could knock me down with a feather if RHF are deployed to the Gulf.'

In our eyes God had spoken. The CO knew things that other people didn't. I mean, he was the head man. So if he said we weren't going, that was it, finished, no fucking questions asked. Boy, was I fucking happy that there was no war for us. More importantly, I would be able to buy myself out in about five months' time. Things were looking good, I would live a normal life pretty soon, no more air disasters and no more death. Yeah, that would be great.

We spent the following four weeks as duty company; that involved doing camp guard and providing people for various small exercises that the battalion was committed to. This was a fairly quiet period, which was almost enjoyable and gave us a chance to settle back into some kind of routine. It was the proverbial lull before the storm and things would never be as good again.

During Christmas leave that year, I received a phone call from my unit and, guess what? I had to report back to Cambridge straightaway for build-up training, we were going to the Gulf. So much for the CO's bullshit talk. We were going to war, what a way to bring in the new year.

In true, loyal squaddie fashion, I reported back to camp the next day, unsure of what lay ahead. As I walked through the camp, I noticed some of the trucks and Land Rovers had already been painted in desert camouflage. It was only then that I fully realised the seriousness of what was going on. This was going to be an armed conflict, it wasn't some poxy exercise on Salisbury Plain, this was fucking war.

Until then I didn't know much about war but of one thing I was sure: people die or should I say people are killed, people just like you and me. Deep down I really thought the politicians would have sorted everything out before we reached Saudi Arabia, but this was more wishful thinking than anything else.

I didn't feel scared. There was no need to be, after all, things would be back to normal in a few weeks. It was my turn to be wrong, the war wheels were well and truly in motion.

Civvy street looked further and further away. I would have to stay in the army until this conflict was over. Incredibly, the army still wanted me to go and try for my officer training but I wasn't interested, it was hard enough just being a squaddie.

We all launched into a very strict training regime and it was bloody hard work. A lot of time was spent on NBC warfare. Subjects that had seemed dull before now became very important, as it could mean the difference between life and death. First-aid training was also quite high on the agenda, once again we all listened carefully. In between lectures we were also given lots of injections, but no one told us what most of them were for. We didn't need to know, apparently, which is just as well, as the truth would have caused a full-scale mutiny amongst the troops. Years later we were to find out that some of the vaccines were not even licensed for use in the UK at that time.

We were issued with some new items of kit, which included the long-awaited PLCE (personal load-carrying equipment) and six NBC suits each. It was obviously thought that chemical weapons would be a very real threat to us. A lot of emphasis was put on the practical side of NBC training and our drills had to be very slick and almost second nature to all of us. Most of the battalion were training about 12 hours a day and it was like being back at the training depot, only fucking worse.

A few days later we found out what our primary role would be. All the regimental officers had known for days beforehand, but they didn't tell us because of the security implications. Well, that was the reason they gave us, which, like everything else, was bullshit. I later found out the real reason: it was because they couldn't trust us, they thought we would leak information to the press. That really pissed me off, we were about to go to war and already they were keeping our balls on the line, risking life and limb. Anyway, our main task in the Gulf would be as a PWGF (prisoner-of-war guard force), consisting of us and two other infantry regiments. It was hardly a top-secret role.

The following week the battalion travelled to Salisbury Plain training area. It was fucking freezing and I have never been so cold in my life. We spent four days practising live section attacks, crawling around in the mud and check-zeroing our rifles. We worked bloody hard, although we had a good incentive. The fact that we would soon be at war certainly helped us switch on. For me, personally, I didn't care. My spirit had been well and truly broken. During the day I was an infantry soldier and at night I was, well, I don't really know – the only words I can think of are desperate, depressed and fucked up.

Back at camp our platoon commander handed each of us a form. This was not unusual, the army has forms for everything. 'Fill them in now and then hand straight back in,' he said, leaving the room sharpish. I studied the form carefully; it was a will.

'Why are we getting these?' someone asked.

'To make paper aeroplanes – you fucking dickhead!' said the platoon sergeant entering the room. 'Right, gather round and sign for these.'

One by one we were issued with ID discs, more commonly known as dog-tags. The sergeant then explained that the smaller chain and tag were actually for putting on our bodybags, that really cheered us up. For the first time we started to realise that some of us, or indeed all of us, might not come back alive. It was a sobering thought.

That afternoon we departed on coaches for our final leave before flying out to Saudi Arabia. My four days were spent visiting various members of my family. It was an emotional time and I couldn't help wondering if I would ever see them again. However, I put a brave face on and pretended everything was great, after all, this was my job, war is what we ultimately trained for. As a child I had longed for a career in the army, it was my dream and, as far as I was concerned, it was the army or nothing. Given the choice now, it would be the nothing. My lifelong ambition was starting to be my downfall, never in my wildest dreams could I have imagined how things would turn out.

After leave was over, we carried out some last-minute

preparations, such as packing kit and attending several lectures on desert navigation. We were also given more injections and my arm was starting to resemble a pin-cushion. At roll-call one morning, the sergeant-major asked if anyone had a motorbike licence. Without even thinking about it, I stepped forward. 'Come and see me straight after this, Donnan,' he said.

'Yes, sir,' I replied.

In truth I had never even sat on a motorbike in my life, let alone held a licence. During my career the army had told me plenty of lies, it was now my turn to tell a couple. It wasn't a big lie, anyway, just a small white lie, the ones that everybody tells now and again. Why did I do it? I don't have a clue, maybe I was going mad, as a few people had started to point out, but it seemed like a good idea at the time. I must have lied well as the sergeant-major gave me the job. My full title was company motorcycle dispatch rider. All I had to worry about was learning to ride a motorbike and the fact that there wasn't a motorbike for miles certainly didn't help. I had to settle for a pretend one while a mate talked me through how to drive. We went through everything from starting the engine to changing gears. I didn't have a fucking clue.

The United Nations deadline had now passed and the coalition forces had authorisation to use all necessary measures to eject Saddam's forces from Kuwait. War was only hours away.

On a cold, dreary morning we boarded a Kuwaiti Airlines 747. I wasn't too happy about our choice of aircraft, the last time I had seen a jumbo jet had been at Lockerbie. Four hours later we landed at Dhahran. As I walked down the aircraft steps I noticed two things: the heat and the amount of military hardware – it was like something from a war movie. There were rows and rows of attack helicopters, fighter aircraft and bombers. All this hardware had one purpose in life – to kill people. Yet it was almost awe-inspiring to see this amount of aircraft on one airfield. I can remember thinking: 'Thank fuck I'm not an Iraqi, poor bastards.'

We were all shuffled on to buses for the road move to Al-Jubayl. Our luggage consisted of a helmet and a respirator, this was in case we came under attack en route, good thinking someone. This was short-lived, however, because the bus was overcrowded with squaddies. If we had been attacked, none of us could have even moved, never mind put a gas mask on. At one point it looked like we wouldn't even reach the battlefield alive as the bus driver was a fucking madman. Someone shouted that he probably worked for the Iraqi secret police and we all laughed. Throughout the bus journey we all presumed our bus driver couldn't speak English, so we sat behind him and discussed his driving skills. We agreed that he was a fucking suicidal maniac. As we approached our destination in the port of Al-Jubayl, the driver turned to us and laughed. 'Fuck off, you Scottish wankers!' was all he said, in better English than most of us could speak.

Our accommodation for a few days was a new camp built for immigrant workers. We were lucky as some of the other regiments had been put in Baldrick lines, a tented transit camp. I had just started unpacking my kit when an alarm sounded.

'What the fuck is that?' someone asked.

'Fuck knows,' I answered.

As I looked around the room, I noticed everyone else was taking cover under beds and hiding in cupboards. It was like something from *Dad's Army*, with none of us having a clue what we were supposed to be doing. After about ten minutes the alarm stopped; it turned out to be a Scud warning. So much for being professional.

That night I had my final practice on my 'ghost bike'. Everything was going well, or so I thought. In the morning I would sign for my new motorbike, then would come the moment of truth. Only a couple of mates knew the true story and one had even bet a free afternoon's drinking if I pulled it off. That was a good incentive. The only problem was that we were in Saudi Arabia where drinking was forbidden by law.

After breakfast I paraded at the motor transport office. I was shitting myself, what had I done? I even thought about owning up to my lie, but then I remembered the MTWO (motor transport warrant officer) would probably punch my face in; he had quite a reputation for being a hard man. I walked into the office and halted beside his desk.

'Where is your licence, Donnan?' he asked.

'Eh, em, I've left it in the UK, sir,' I lied.

'You fucking what?' he said, starting to get angry.

'No one told me to bring it, sir.'

'You are a dickhead – sign here, take the keys and fuck off,' he said, looking disgusted. I scribbled my signature on the form and hurried out of the office. 'Donnan, get back in here,' he shouted at the top of his voice.

'Yes, sir.'

'That bike is your responsibility. One fucking thing goes wrong with it and you're charged.'

'Yes, sir, don't worry, sir,' I said, flapping.

Around the corner was my motorbike and, like all good army equipment it was green and shiny, it looked out of place considering every other vehicle was in desert colours. I stood and stared at it. According to the log book it had done only 50 miles and there wasn't a scratch on it. I made sure no one was about and climbed on then I put the key in the ignition and kick-started the engine. For about two minutes I sat there revving the throttle. Eventually I found the courage to put the bike into gear and let out the clutch. The bike lurched forward and gathered speed and all I could do was hang on. At the point of impact I was doing a wheelie, unintentionally, of course. I had hit a parked Land Rover head on and the crunching of metal and my screams had attracted some attention. I was unhurt but the bike had suffered some damage. The MTWO nearly had a fit. 'You are a fucking wanker,' he was saying.

'Yes, Colour, I don't know what happened.'

'You better get a fucking grip, son – do you understand?'

It was more of a statement than a question. After that incident the MTWO hated me, although at the time I couldn't understand what I had done wrong. That afternoon three other dispatch riders and I loaded our bikes on to a truck and headed to the helipad near the port in Al-Jubayl. After much fucking around by myself, I slowly learned how to ride a motorbike. Three hours later, I drove the bike back to camp. I thought I was Steve McQueen in *The Great Escape*. Had I bothered to look at the speedo I wouldn't have been so cocky. I was travelling at a speed of 20 miles an hour, hardly any comparison to the great man himself.

Next morning, I was given a huge tin of sand-coloured paint and I was ordered to paint five bikes as punishment for crashing the bike. I thought that was not a bad deal considering the circumstances. The sun was shining, it was a glorious day and I was almost happy for a few hours, then I remembered what we were here for, to fight a bloody war. For the last four years my army training had been all about war, now it was happening it just seemed like yet another exercise with mock scenarios. I had spent the last four years pretending about a make-believe enemy, now I was pretending the real enemy was false. Boy, was I mixed up!

At the beginning of February we moved as a company to makeshift ranges in the desert. For a day I practised live firing and trench clearing. I fired more live rounds that day than I had in my entire army career. The heat in the desert was incredible, as T.E. Lawrence once said: 'The heat of Arabia came out like a drawn sword and struck us speechless.' I couldn't have put it better myself! At night the temperature dropped rapidly, in fact it was brass monkey's stuff and our desert combats were woefully inadequate for the job in hand. However, like all good infantry soldiers we improvised, and our NBC suits soon became our pyjamas.

We travelled back to camp for the last time as soon we would deploy deeper into the desert and start playing the waiting game. We called this 'on the bus, off the bus'; they would tell us one thing, then five minutes later it would be changed. I'll give you an example. Our new-issue army webbing was bright green, everything in the desert is a sandy colour, hence we would stand out – which is not a good idea if someone is shooting at you. It went against every rule we had ever been taught regarding camouflage and concealment. We would have been as well wearing bright red T-shirts with the logo 'Please shoot me'. So our quartermaster-sergeant (QMS) told us to splash some desert paint over the kit. We raced off to find paint and a brush. I couldn't find either, but a couple of the lads had scrounged paint from the MT (motor transport) platoon and they had just started painting when, right on cue, the battalion quartermaster (QM) appeared. 'Stop what you're doing right fucking now! Who told you to do this?' he asked, trembling with rage.

'Our QMS, sir,' one of the Jocks replied.

'Do you know how much this fucking costs?'

'No, sir.'

All he was worried about was the equipment, it didn't matter that it could help save our lives. Today, if I met that horrible man, I would have one question to ask him: 'Do you really care more about the webbing than the people who are wearing it?' Maybe he was unwell, war does funny things to people. It could have been something to do with the tablets we were swallowing for most of the fucking day, strange little pills called NAPS (nerve agent pre-treatment sets). They had never been given to personnel under a chemical warfare threat before. Never once did anyone provide adequate information about the tablets and we were given no opportunity to accept or decline the treatment. We were more or less ordered to take them and, like the obedient soldier I was, I took the pills and never asked any questions. Me and the rest of the British Army. How trusting we once were! Given the chance now, I would crush the pills up and put them in tea. Anyone for tea, old chap? The most deserving of a cup of tea would be the ex-Armed Forces Minister Nicholas Soames and most of his staff at the Ministry of Defence, and some, not all, of the army top brass. If there were any left over then I'm sure we could spare some for old Saddam Hussein. One thing, though, it would have to be in that particular order. As in the army, everything goes on merit!

On 16 February we moved as a battalion to a holding area just outside Al-Qaysumah. We spent a couple of nights in Maryhill camp. This was a specially converted PoW compound, built by our very own assault pioneer platoon. The camp was divided into three separate compounds, each one capable of holding around 2,000 prisoners. Around the compounds was a huge sand berm – a wall of sand pushed into place by bulldozers which created a high obstacle and ensured that the prisoners couldn't see what was going on – intertwined with some nasty-looking razor wire, and overlooking each area was a large, sandbagged watchtower, complete with floodlights. It looked like something from a Second World War movie, the only thing we didn't have were prisoners-of-war. All good things come to he who waits! So that's what we did, for days we waited patiently for some kind of news. We were in the dark. People back home were better informed of the general picture. The only information we were passed was that if a full-scale ground war did start, we could expect 15,000 casualties on the first day alone. What a fucking waste; we were all going to die. That night, for the third time in my life, I prayed: forgive them, Father, for they know not what they do. Or maybe it should be 'they don't give a fuck what they do'. A bit blasphemous maybe, but that was how I really did feel. First it had been Lockerbie, then Cloyd's death in Belize and now this stupid fucking war. When would all this madness end? When would all the nightmares go away? When would I be me again? I was so tired, all I wanted was to lie down and sleep for a while, or maybe forever.

After three nights in Maryhill camp, we travelled 70 kilometres to yet another range somewhere in the desert. Here we fought our first battle – with the sand. It was something that we hadn't given much thought to. But soon we were eating food with a layer of sand on top and then there was my arse, it was rubbed raw; sand in the crack of your arse is pretty sore, believe me. Our personal weapons were rendered almost useless and, no matter how often they were cleaned, sand always clogged up the working parts. To be fair, the rifle was a pile of shite; in a battle it would have been good for only one thing – throwing at the enemy. That was how much faith most of us had in our SA80s.

During the day, while everyone else was doing live firing, I spent hours driving around on my bike, trying to look as if I knew what I was doing. After two more spectacular crashes, I began to feel more confident and driving the bike across the flat, featureless desert soon became a welcome release from the pressures of life.

Rumours started doing the rounds. We heard that droves of the Iraqi Army were surrendering to the Allies, if true, this could only be good news. We also learned that the coalition aircraft had been bombing the Iraqi front line since the day we left England. This was a systematic plan designed to reduce their combat effectiveness by almost half. We chose to believe both rumours.

At night I would lie shivering in my sleeping bag, and often I could see large formations of Allied aircraft forming up and heading towards the border. I was jealous of the aircrew, I imagined them sitting in their nice heated cockpits, all they had to do was drop a few bombs, then they could fuck off back

My passing-out parade at Glencorse Barracks, Edinburgh.
That's me in the centre

ABOVE: the helipad where I waited anxiously
for news of Private Cloyd Gillet (G. HOPE)
LEFT: typical army accommodation in Belize
(G. HOPE)
BELOW: ready for action during the Gulf War

ABOVE: cleaning our weapons and battling against our biggest enemy: the sand
RIGHT: the remains of tanks and other vehicles littering the road to Kuwait after the Allied bombing raids
(COURTESY M.S. POWER)

ABOVE: catching some rays
LEFT: me in the Saudi desert just hours before the ground attack

to some plush hotel in Dhahran. I was in the wrong job!

Morale was at an all-time low with the lads. There were a number of reasons for this. Food being the first reason, it was quite simple, we hardly got any. If an army marches on its stomach, then I reckoned we would get about half a mile. The second reason was the amount of bullshit we had to endure, loads and loads of it. Day after day it was kit inspections, followed by rifle inspections. Some mornings our boots were checked by one of the senior NCOs. 'We might be at war, but that's no excuse for having fucking dirty boots,' one of them said. The regiment's insistence on petty discipline caused us all great anguish, some of us even joked that on our return to the UK we would join the army; a real regiment, commanded by people with brains and common sense. Many soldiers were now beginning to see the regiment for what it really was.

Some time after the war a brave soldier from our regiment designed a T-shirt. On the front was a large mushroom, standing underneath it was a small soldier, dressed in uniform. It said: 'Mushroom Battalion. Kept in the dark and fed on shit.' We were all delighted, in our eyes it was a work of art. However, as usual, the hierarchy were not impressed and they promptly banned us from wearing the T-shirts.

On 21 February we moved back to the holding area at Al-Qaysumah, where we were given the news that we were on G-3. 'G' stood for go-day, so, obviously, the ground assault would begin in three days' time. Preparations started straightaway and we cleaned our rifles like they had never been cleaned before, while respirators and NBC suits were checked, magazines emptied and each bullet was wiped clean and then carefully replaced. We even sharpened our bayonets, which also doubled as wirecutters, handy for cutting through razor wire which is almost always placed near trenches. Although our primary role was guarding prisoners-of-war, we had to be prepared for every eventuality. As we sat in small groups cleaning our weapons that afternoon, another rumour reached our ears. This time it was more serious; we were told that the NAPS tablets which we were scoffing daily made you sterile. We were prepared to face the wrath of Saddam Hussein, but taking tablets that fucked up your family allowance was downright dangerous. I promptly buried mine in the sand and vowed never to touch another tablet of any kind.

That day was like many others in the Gulf: cleaning weapons, bullshitting each other, sitting about in the sun and having a good moan. No different, except for one thing: we now knew that war was on a strict timetable and in under 72 hours the ground battle would begin. A day that should stick in your memory forever, wouldn't you think? Yet, I have tried to recall many times how I felt that day, in truth I don't remember, it has gone from my memory as if it were never there. Perhaps I felt nothing, maybe I was numb and in shock and all that. In truth, I was shitting myself. The only reason I know this is from reading a letter I sent back home. My inability to remember events that day has caused me much anguish. I have a couple of theories. Could it have been something to do with those tablets? Or maybe I was so mentally ill my mind had just closed down. Whatever the reasons, it should never have happened. It was wrong. The whole fucking thing was wrong, we were in the wrong place doing the wrong things. Others made the decisions and we lived with the consequences.

The following night I was alone on duty in the command post, it was the early hours of the morning and I could hear explosions in the distance, I was cold and tired. Several times I got up and jogged on the spot in a vain attempt to keep myself awake. My job was to monitor the radios and the nuclear–chemical detection equipment for any sign of activity. With the exception of the distant shelling, things were generally quiet. At 0200 hours the silence of the tent was abruptly broken, pulling me from my comatose state. The chemical-agent monitor was showing a particularly high reading, instinctively I reached for my respirator. I quickly pulled the mask over my face and shouted the magic words: 'GAS – GAS – GAS!' Immediately, I sounded the air horns. This was the standard signal to alert everyone nearby. Within minutes the tent was crowded with every senior NCO and his dog arriving to find out if the alarm was for real. At that point I was invited to fuck off outside. I awkwardly crawled inside my bed for the night: a hastily dug hole in the sand. Sleep never came easy. Have you tried to sleep in a sand-hole, wearing a mask and an NBC suit, wondering if you're going to die a horrific death from chemical weapons?

At dawn, after nearly six hours 'masked up', we were given the all-clear. According to my boss, it had been a false alarm. In his words, the highly calibrated device was activated by a low-flying aircraft. He forgot one thing: I was on duty at the time and there were no low-flying aircraft that night. Someone was telling lies once more.

We spent that day doing final things. I penned my letters back home, to people I loved. I wrote that after the war was over, I would be a different person, more honest, more caring and more understanding, I would be a better person for my experiences and never again would I hurt anyone, all the mistakes I had made would be put right. This also turned out to be a lie. Almost straightaway I was put to the test by the MTWO, who had developed a deep and meaningful hatred of me. I suppose in his eyes I was a wanker who couldn't ride a motorbike. Anyway, the MTWO was a colour sergeant whom I shall call BFA (big, fat arsehole). My job was to accompany him, both of us on bikes, to a camp a few miles away. We set off at a fairly slow speed and not a word was spoken between us. BFA was even slower on a bike than I was, in fact, he was scared. I, meantime, was loving it. I opened the throttle and sped quickly away from Fatty. He didn't want to lose face, so, reluctantly, he tried to catch me. I was in my glory, loving every minute of his fear, revenge is sweet. When we arrived at the camp, Fatty sat on the bike shaking. He told me a secret: he had never held a motorbike licence either.

'Really, Colour?' I replied, wondering if I should let him in on my little lie. For a couple of minutes he was almost human, in fact, he was nearly likeable.

'Hold these till I get off,' said BFA, handing me his helmet and gloves. What happened next was my happiest memory of the Gulf War. Talk about laugh, I couldn't move. It made sure Fatty would hate me forever. Climbing off the bike he had some trouble, his leg was too lardy to lift over the bike. Not only that, his belly was in the way. Eventually, after plenty of fucking around, he lifted his leg back and up and over the whole bike, at the same time catching his boot on the luggage straps. As he pulled, the bike fell on top of him.

'Fucking help – get the bike off me – don't just stand there.' I was happy, the MTWO's dignity had gone, he looked like an upturned turtle flopping about. I wanted to laugh in his face. What goes around comes around. 'Tell anyone about this and you're for it,' he was ranting. 'Do you understand?'

'Yes, Colour,' I replied, trying hard not to laugh too much.

We both travelled the short distance back to Al-Qaysumah, on the wrong side of the road, the blind leading the blind. My first mission was to find a senior member of the motor transport platoon, who all hated BFA more than I did. As you have gathered by now, I can't keep secrets very well. Once the appropriate 'mole' was found I leaked the story. Fair is fair, well, at least I think so.

That night the rain started, and within hours the desert had changed into a muddy quagmire. The weather was well timed. Maybe the powers that be had some way of controlling the rainfall, maybe it was all part of a plan designed to lower the morale of the Iraqis. Coincidence maybe, but clever all the same. At 0400 hours that morning, as we lay snoring, the French 6th Division and the US 82nd Airborne smashed through enemy defences into Iraq. The ground war had begun, for some troops anyway.

As daylight broke, on a wet miserable morning, we gathered at the mess tent for our scoff. We quickly shoved the food down our necks as it was so crap we didn't want to taste it. We stood in small groups and moaned, mainly about life, particularly life in the Royal Highland Fusiliers. We agreed it was as shit as the food we scoffed; we loved moaning. Apparently, the senior ranks within the regiment had a saying that if we Jocks weren't moaning then something really was wrong. The conversation then turned to killing people, not the Iraqis, as you would imagine, but prominent people within the regiment. First to be shot, by a unanimous decision, would be the cook, followed by a couple of nasty platoon sergeants. One of the lads then produced a bullet from his webbing, it had been filed slightly, for maximum effect. 'This one is for that cunt,' he said, pointing to a junior NCO who was standing nearby. We had been joking, but this mental bastard was deadly serious. I had no doubt, if given the chance, he would put a bullet in the NCO's back. Who needs enemies when you have friends like that?

By late afternoon we had still heard nothing about the ground attack and many of us were starting to get impatient. This was the hardest part, the waiting and the not knowing, but that's how it goes. An infantryman's life is either periods of intense activity or sitting about doing fuck all.

The driving rain continued well into the night. I crawled into my hole in the sand once more, wriggled into my sleeping bag and tried to shut out the world. Sleep was interrupted continually. At one point I was told to get the bike and head to the CO's tent. It was pitch-dark, the rain was almost horizontal and I was like a zombie, a lethal combination. For tactical reasons I couldn't use the headlights on the bike so, basically, it was like driving blind. For 20 minutes I drove around in circles, lost, well, not lost, no one ever gets lost in the army, I just didn't know where I was. Next thing I'm in a six-foot hole, me and the bike. It turned out to be someone's fire trench. Luckily for them it was unoccupied. It took six unhappy soldiers to haul the bike back out and I never did make the CO's tent. Next morning there were problems, big fucking problems. We had no communications between us and the PWGF headquarters. We were in the dark and without comms we could do nothing as accurate information was needed to ensure everyone was in the right place at the right time.

This reminded me of a story I had once heard during my signals course. The scene is set in the trenches of the First World War, a British regiment was about to go over the top, a message was to be passed beforehand, by word of mouth, down through the various networks. 'Send reinforcements – we are going to advance.' When the message finally reached the ears of those it was intended for, it had changed somewhat. 'Send three and fourpence – we are going to a dance.' True or not, I don't know, but a good example of how things can easily become confused, especially in the heat of battle.

Some tosser in Battalion HQ decided we should move forward on our own initiative, up the main supply route nicknamed 'Dodge'. This was not a good idea, in fact, it was fucking stupid. Basically, we ambled along, totally oblivious to the war. This was typical of the RHF, so full of its own self-importance, we didn't need orders, we didn't need comms, let us just go somewhere, anywhere. Since the Gulf I have studied many books written about the war and all talk about the slick manoeuvres and the precision timings. That may be so for the armoured regiments, but we were more like sloths, only not as fast.

That night we discovered that we had moved too far forward and we were now ahead of the DAA (divisional administration area) and the other two battalions who belonged to the PWGF. We received our first bit of news via the BBC World Service, that Allied troops had halted some 30 miles short of Kuwait City and were poised to retake it. Even better was the news that Allied casualties were remarkably light. Thousands of Iraqis had surrendered, many were stunned by the ferocity of the onslaught. The armoured brigades had done well.

Nothing had changed for us, we were still waiting patiently in the fucking, pissing rain. As the rain poured from the sky, I stripped off and had my first proper wash in days. The weather depressed us greatly for two reasons: firstly, we got wet and secondly, it reminded us so much of home. Scotland and rain go hand in hand. Home seemed a million miles away, would I ever see it again?

Fourteen hours later we crossed the border into Iraq which was marked with a huge sand berm, nearly three metres tall. Someone had made a shoddy-looking sign, obviously done by the Yanks, 'Iraq this way', underneath it was a huge arrow. The terrain changed abruptly, it became rocky and the sand was more like gravel. This, coupled with the rain, made the motorbike very difficult to control. Several times that day I crashed, twice I was nearly killed. The first incident happened as I stopped for a short break. There I was, sitting minding my own business, when literally out of nowhere an American tank appeared, heading straight for me and, worse still, the fucking thing was in reverse. The vision of 60 tonnes of tank hurtling towards you at 30 miles an hour does things to you. I ran like a world-class sprinter for a few seconds, luckily it missed me and the bike, with only a few feet to spare. The second incident happened later that night and it was entirely my fault. It was dark, we were driving as a convoy through the minefield breeches, which is basically a lane cleared of any mines by the engineers which allows us to drive through safely. The safe area was well marked out with tape and luminous arrows and either side of that lay many thousands of mines, all hidden. Almost halfway through we stopped, I climbed off the bike and stretched my legs. I had been driving for nearly 16 hours, most of the time in zero visibility and heavy rain. I was tired. 'Dispatch rider to the front,' shouted the signals NCO from the comfort of his Land Rover. I jumped on the bike, kick-started it into life and gingerly rode to the front, where I met the CO and RSM (regimental sergeant-major) standing outside their Land Rover, both looked exhausted.

'Right Donnan, listen in – when the convoy sets off again, I want you to stay at the rear and check for any stragglers, understood?' said the commanding officer.

'Yes, sir.'

'Oh, and make sure everyone stays tight together.'

'Okay, sir,' I said kicking the bike into gear. Without thinking, I turned in a huge circle. My mind clicked once I was on the minefield, by then it was too late. Time slowed down.

'Get out of there, you fucking idiot!' That was the RSM, warning me. You should have seen the look on his face. Mind you, he probably said the same about me. My life didn't flash in front of me but thoughts of being blown to pieces did. I opened the throttle and tried to be nonchalant about the whole thing, as if it was something you do every day. Fortunately for me, and my arse, I made it back to the safe lane in one piece. I had been in the danger area for maybe only 30 seconds, but I was lucky. For my troubles I received a severe bollocking from the company sergeant-major (CSM), just what I needed.

We carried on driving till just after midnight when the whole regiment had now cleared the minefield breech safely. Priority was now to get some sleep. We hastily set up camouflage nets over the vehicles and dug small shell scrapes in the hard ground. It was bitterly cold, the sky was clear, thousands of stars were visible, something was different, then it dawned on me, the rain had stopped for the first time in a few days. Shortly afterwards, we heard that Kuwait had been liberated. This was good news, the war wouldn't last much longer. People smiled, we were happy, life didn't seem that bad.

I zipped up my sleeping bag and slept the sleep of the dead.

Five hours later it was time to move. After a cold breakfast we repacked the cam nets and sorted out our vehicles. It was a glorious day, the sun was shining. The atmosphere had changed, it was more relaxed, we were all going to live. 'Ready to move,' came the order. The convoy slowly gathered speed as we moved into our order of march, CO's Land Rover and HQ Company at the front, followed by A Company, B Company, C Company, and then Fire-Support Company. On each side of the convoy would be two motorbike outriders to make sure the convoy stayed together.

The sheer devastation soon became apparent as we cleared the other vehicles. Burnt-out tank hulls lay scattered across the desert, empty trench systems stood almost ghostlike, a few discarded possessions lay nearby, almost engulfed by the sand. I later found out that many of the Iraqis had simply been buried alive inside their trench systems, drowned in the sand. As I weaved over the terrain, the bike struck something, or should I say someone. It was a dead man, he was one of them. His body was riddled with bullet holes, his brain was now on the outside of his head, halfway down his face to be precise. Death had not been glorious. Lifeless, dead, they were the enemy, weren't they?

I moved further on back towards the convoy and I nearly bumped into more dead enemy, it was becoming an occupational hazard. All around were bodies, all shapes and sizes, some bodies had no legs, others had no arms, there were bits and pieces everywhere. They had two things in common, all had moustaches and all were fucking dead, blown to oblivion. Maybe a moustache was part of the uniform. Strange the things you notice when all around you are corpses. I realised something, the dead enemy were dead people who once loved, laughed and lived. Just like me and you. It was mindless, barbaric, testosterone-induced slaughter. I tried to convince myself that this was for something – Lockerbie, Cloyd's death

– but this madness was all for nothing. Sheer fucking lunacy!

I have seen what humans can do to each other, it doesn't bear thinking about, it isn't nice. Please believe me, I wouldn't want you or anyone else to go through that. I never prayed that day, it was too late for that, instead I became confused. That was the day I died inside. Nothing mattered anymore, what was the point of anything? We were all going to die. I stopped hoping, despair washed over me. I wanted to run, anywhere, far away from death, insanity and devastation. I set off on the bike, dazed and confused. I don't remember what happened for the next few hours, my mind is blank. The only thing I know for sure is that I became separated from the RHF. The next thing I can recall is meeting a British armoured reconnaissance regiment who offered to put me up for the night. Years later I was to find out that 'battleshock' had caused my memory loss.

Next morning, after a long, lonely night, I travelled back to meet up with my regiment, who were only a few miles away. Surprisingly, no one gave me a bollocking, in fact, only a handful realised I had disappeared. The sergeant-major nicknamed me 'Pathfinder'.

At 0800 hours that morning, the order was given to 'unload'. It was official, the war was over. We cheered, we smiled, we were still alive. For a few minutes overwhelming emotions bonded us together, we were almost as one.

'When are we going home, then?' someone asked.

'Don't ask stupid questions – get your fucking weapons cleaned,' said the colour sergeant.

Then it was gone, back to a them-and-us scenario. We sat around in groups and started to strip our weapons.

'Get your weapons back together, ready to move in ten minutes!' barked the CSM.

Almost immediately a junior NCO started on us: 'Get fucking moving, come on, let's go for it.'

We exchanged a few sideward glances. Wishing those cunts

would disappear became my favourite pastime. Sometimes, when things became too much, I practised in my mind telling the sergeant-major to fuck off, although I never did as I didn't have the bottle.

Soon we were on the move yet again. We travelled east towards the Kuwait–Iraq border. The war may have been over but our work was just beginning. We stopped five miles short of the border and set up a DHA (divisional holding area) and within two hours we had over 2,400 prisoners of war, who had been ferried in by Chinook helicopter. They were in a bad way, some had not eaten in five days. Most were smiling and glad to be alive. See, they were human and, like us, they didn't want to be there. As a priority, we fed and watered them. One thing I did notice was that they were all poorly equipped and one even needed a walking stick, they were hardly fighting machines. Soldiers who had once been our enemy now became our patients. We had strict guidelines to adhere to, it's called the Geneva Convention, this saved their lives. Many trigger-happy soldiers in my regiment would have quite willingly executed them all, just to make things simpler.

The Iraqis also had similar thoughts and soon became very suspicious of the deep latrines we had dug for them. They believed this would be their final resting place. Some even pissed themselves rather than go near the latrines. Large numbers of these Iraqis had also fought in the Iran–Iraq war, so they were no strangers to human atrocities.

We were looking after a Third World army, it had been a ridiculously unequal slaughter. Over the next three days we moved nearer to Kuwait City and all of the PoWs were handed over to various elements of the PWGF.

The aftermath of the war was unbelievable. I don't recall when or where it happened, the horror of it I can clearly remember. We saw dead Iraqis being bulldozed into a hole, not two or three, but hundreds, all stiff with rigor mortis. As I watched in horror I realised that these corpses were fathers, sons and brothers. Now they were dead – finished, gone, lifeless – all for one reason: war. We live in a civilised world, surely the dead should be treated with a bit more respect. I mean, it's not too much to expect, is it? Maybe the world is not as civilised as we like to think. The futility of it all, the waste and the madness, God forgive them because I never will. I was 19, I had seen enough waste to last a lifetime and what really angered me was that none of it should have happened. At the end of the day I ask myself, why? Nearly eight years later I'm still asking the same questions and still I have no answers. It remains as confusing now as it did then. Perhaps one day I'll make sense of it, maybe even understand it.

I witnessed the carnage on Mutla Ridge on 4 March, where the 'turkey shoot' took place. The route was lined with thousands of burnt-out vehicles, all around were black, charred bodies. The Iraqis had tried to retreat from Kuwait to Basra but they hadn't made it. US aircraft bombed them, again and again. So many jets congregated on this area that a mid-air collision was feared and the attack was compared to shooting fish in a barrel.

This was the highway to hell. I have a photograph of a burnt Iraqi, he is sitting inside a truck and, from a distance, he could be mistaken for smiling, but close examination shows the teeth are clenched together in pain and black flesh hangs from his face, or should I say from his skull, as his face is gone, melted on to the floor. Believe it or not he is still holding the steering wheel. I now understand the meaning of 'dust to dust and ashes to ashes'.

War is wrong, war is nothing more than government-sanctioned murder. No man has the right to take another human life. Humans are meant to be the most intelligent species on this planet. You should see what they are capable of doing to each other. It makes you sick.

We returned to Maryhill camp on 5 March and we spent four days guarding 5,000 prisoners-of-war. That was the day I learned an old friend had been killed; not by the Iraqis, as you would imagine, but by a trigger-happy American pilot. He had murdered nine British soldiers – the fucking tosser opened fire on their armoured personnel carrier believing them to be enemy. The army called this 'friendly fire'. It was a mistake, they said. There is no such thing as friendly fire. My friend's death can vouch for that.

Before you go to bed tonight, please close your eyes and think of this, even if it's for only a few seconds, think of all the souls who have given their lives, so you can sleep soundly in your bed. Do it, please.

The war was over, but for me the battle was just beginning. A battle that would take me to the very limits of my physical and mental endurance.

On 8 March we returned to Al-Jubayl, where the war had started. The next four weeks were spent training, cleaning and generally being fucked about. I was given news by the CO: my transfer had come through, after Gulf leave I would report to the Army Air Corps. This was everything I had worked for. I was on my way to becoming an army helicopter pilot but now it meant nothing to me.

Soon we were back in the UK and we all went our separate ways for three weeks' post-Gulf leave. Unknown to me, my career was already over.

6. On the Run

After my three weeks' leave was over, I failed to report for duty. I was AWOL. This wasn't a conscious decision, my subconscious mind had simply taken over. I was, in fact, mentally ill, although at the time I didn't know it. In short, my brain wasn't working at all, it had given up.

Gulf leave had been a nightmare for me and my family. They told me I had changed; maybe so. 'What the fuck do they know about it, anyway?' I thought.

Night became day, daylight was good, night-time was bad, it was evil, I hated the dark, it frightened me. Images of dead Iraqis slaughtered on the battlefield, dead passengers at Lockerbie and poor Cloyd, would sneak into my mind and dreams.

Depression and despair ravaged my body, my temper was on a short fuse and my new hobbies were crying and punching things. Nothing mattered any more, what was the point in anything? We're all going to die anyway, fuck this for a game of soldiers. No one could understand what I was going through, least of all me. One thing was for sure, probably the only thing, I could take no more of the British Army. No more air disasters, no more wars and no more murder inquiries. Enough was enough. My once-beloved regiment now represented a living nightmare. No, I couldn't go back there, they wouldn't understand anyway. At night I would go out walking, strolling along the empty streets alone. I had never experienced such strong emotion in my life. Overwhelming feelings of utter loneliness gripped me, I didn't want to think about my past, never mind talk about it. I hated myself, I couldn't even look at myself in the mirror. On the really bad days I often contemplated killing myself, at least then I would have peace and quiet in my brain. Something always stopped me. I was a coward. I didn't have the balls to top myself, at least not then, anyway. I stopped believing in myself and the rest of the world.

Months later I was to find out that my absence wasn't reported for a week, it was so out of character that the sergeant-major refused to believe it. He actually thought I had been killed travelling back to Cambridge. Even at that point no one thought to find out what was wrong. Me, I didn't care. I was free of the army and what they could put me through. If only things were that simple.

Once a soldier has been AWOL for 28 days, the army then contact the local police, the soldier's name and details are noted and he is then officially classed as an absconder and the police then have the power to apprehend him. The only problem was I didn't want to be apprehended. I have nothing against the police, they do a wonderful job, but to me they represented authority, similar to the army, after all, they all work for the same people. If they wanted me then they would have to catch me. On the morning of my twentieth birthday, I received the first of many visits from the law. It was early morning, I hadn't slept that night, outside the air was still and I felt something wasn't right. I could hear the distant sound of a crackling radio. I listened for a moment before peering between the curtains. Outside were two fat policemen trying to move stealthily towards their target. I was, in fact, the target. Quickly I went into my sister's room and shook her awake.

'It's the fucking cops, go and answer the door while I hide,' I whispered, trying to stay calm.

Aynslie left the room and answered the door. Meantime, I squeezed into a tiny upright cupboard. Panic then set in as I realised my birthday cards were out on display. I could do nothing. I could hear muffled snippets of the conversation between the police and my sister.

'Do you mind if we look around?' asked the officer.

'Oh fuck,' I thought. From then on life became worse. The visits slowly increased as the days passed. The police were not going to give up easily, but neither was I. All I wanted was to be left alone. I was sick, I wasn't doing any harm. All I needed was time to sort myself out, get things back in order, then maybe everything would go away. My head was sore, buzzing almost, it felt like hundreds of ants crawling round inside my head. God, it hurt. Why me? Someone please help, make me understand this mental torture, make it stop. God, give me strength, please.

One of the first things to break under the strain was the relationship with my family. In their eyes I had disgraced myself, they were ashamed of me. But that was all right, I was ashamed of me. They just couldn't understand why I had become so strange and aggressive. I never tried to explain. The only advice they gave me was to 'go back to the army and sort it out', which made me feel even worse; it just proved they didn't understand.

The next major catastrophe was money. I didn't have any, I was absolutely skint. This was something I had not accounted for. The police were now visiting my home at all hours, often as many as eight times a day. I became really good at hide-and-seek. I had turns at hiding behind every piece of furniture in the house.

My long walks all night now ceased as it had become too risky. Instead, I would sit in the bedroom gazing at the wallpaper. Life had become an endless round of crying, hiding, and trying hard to forget things. All I can remember thinking is that no one told me it would be so hard – life, that is. Soon my only reactions were to the word 'police' or on hearing a loud knock on the door. Life really was a pile of shite, the whole thing was now spiralling wildly out of control. Where did the army come into this? They didn't. Not once did they attempt to find out my whereabouts. So much for the big family that would always look after me. They were all showing their true colours now.

I was so tired, my zest for life had gone. I couldn't smile, even my sense of humour had vanished. Life was so unfair, or was this all my fault? Had I contributed in some way to this state of affairs, I wonder? It seemed as if it was Barry Donnan versus the world and that everyone had it in for me. I often thought, 'What have I done to deserve this?' I could come to no conclusion. Maybe this was normal, I just didn't have any answers.

I do know one thing, I was hurting inside so much the pain was almost physical. Lack of sleep made me very explosive. On two separate occasions I grabbed close members of my family by the throat. I didn't know what I was doing. Often I would snap for the least reason, rage would consume my body and anything that was around me would be punched. I was uncontrollable, I was like a wild animal let loose. Once I had calmed down, guilt would take over. I was so ashamed.

Then the pain in my head would start and fear, anxiety, anger, guilt, depression would flash through my body. On really bad days it felt as if my head would quite literally explode into a thousand pieces. This was just wishful thinking on my part, I wasn't going to be that lucky. My view of the world was very disturbed when the dark clouds were upon me. Tears would often roll down my face, sometimes I would cry like a baby for no apparent reason, but it didn't help. The wounds were invisible, but I was severely injured. My brain had been polluted with tragedy, murder and the slaughter of plenty of innocent people. I lived with their faces, day and night. I would die soon, where or when I didn't know, but it would be soon, I was sure of that.

At home, things became so grim that I had to leave before I seriously hurt my family, both emotionally and physically. For three nights I lived rough in a local forest, wandering aimlessly at night. I would sleep for a couple of hours during daylight, curled up in the foetal position and pretending the world didn't exist. Solitude was best, then I could hurt no one. My nourishment consisted of a Mars Bar and a fizzy drink per day. The spiral tightened and with each new day the deterioration continued, I was out of my mind.

Next thing, I was living as a squatter. At the time I wasn't complaining, it was a roof over my head. It wasn't exactly the fucking Hilton, the tiny flat contained nothing, not even a carpet, but, as they say, beggars can't be choosers. In a matter of weeks I transformed from a professional soldier (I hate those words) to a fully-fledged tramp, my self-dignity crumbled.

The local cops soon found out. They must have been delighted, my squat was less than a mile from the police station so the visits doubled, as did my paranoia. I hardly left the flat during the day as there was just too much chance of being caught. The safest option was to move under the cover of darkness, or to wait till the shift changed over, I knew the times off by heart. It wasn't safe to use the front door, instead I would climb out the window, from there I could reach a drainpipe and I would carefully climb down past the other two levels. This really annoyed the neighbours who would be quite innocently washing their dishes or eating dinner as I would climb past the window. Worse still, I would wave at them, as if it was the most normal activity on earth. Going back up was even harder, and in weeks to come I wouldn't have the strength to haul myself up, due to malnutrition. Food, or the lack of it, became a serious problem. I was hungry all the time, I hadn't eaten a decent meal in many days. My bodyweight decreased very quickly, almost two stone in a month, things really were getting out of hand. The fact that no one seemed to care certainly didn't help matters. I was well and truly on my own. Looking back, I realise one thing, I was quite literally fighting for my life, for what it was worth.

One afternoon I decided to be brave, don't ask why. Anyway, I handed myself into the local army careers office. 'Sergeant, I'm from 1 RHF – I've been AWOL since the beginning of May,' I explained. I half-expected him to jump up and place steel shackles on me and then throw me in some cupboard, maybe even give me a good bollocking.

'Eh, look mate, it's nearly lunchtime, come back later on.'

'I will do,' I said, already halfway out the door. At that moment I decided, rightly or wrongly, that fate had intervened; I would never go back.

No money, no food, but I had a cunning plan though: I would rob a bank. My thoughts and actions were becoming irrational. Desperate times called for desperate measures.

During the day I started getting flashbacks of particular events. It was like someone switching on a video recorder inside your head. Suddenly you were there again, events going on as I stood helpless, just as I had always done. For seconds, sometimes minutes, my body was not my own. The adrenalin would rush through my system, my heart would beat like never before and sweat would soak my clothes. When it passed, weakness took over, I was tired and drained. Each flashback seemed to take more and more out of me. Once that passed it was sore head time. On occasions the pain became so much I would start punching myself on the head; surprisingly enough, this never helped, it was just sheer frustration and anger.

Who was I? What was I? To be honest I didn't care, life was just a big game, we are the players, everything is controlled and utilised. Basically, we are being used, then, guess what? You fucking die. It's a sick joke. The whole thing is fucked up.

At that point someone, I don't remember who, said I should go and see a doctor. I was quite willing to try anything. I wanted to be normal again. Over a couple of visits the doctor diagnosed PTSD (post-traumatic stress disorder). I had never even heard of it. The doctor, only a little more knowledgeable than me, ordered me to see a shrink.

The psychiatrist was not a pretty sight and he looked in a worse state than I was. Not only that, he was almost blind, he had a pair of milk-bottle-thick glasses on and when he started writing I nearly fell off my chair. The glasses obviously weren't strong enough, so to help him he had a large magnifying glass, then he would push his face right down, almost in the fucking paper. It was rather difficult to take him seriously. Anyway, he too diagnosed PTSD. He advised me to return to the army and face my problems head on. 'Fuck off!' I told him, and with that I left his office.

Outside lay my transport, a racing bike with two flat tyres. It took almost five hours to cycle the ten miles back to the squat. It never occurred to me at the time, but I did get some strange looks that day.

After much deliberating, I decided to hand myself in, maybe the army would understand. Things couldn't really get any worse, could they? After collecting a travel warrant from the army careers office, I boarded the train bound for London. It was the most frightening journey of my life. I was shit scared but, above all, I tried to remain hopeful. In my mental state I was deluding myself, I was living in fairyland.

At Cambridge railway station I was met by a member of the regiment who escorted me back to camp. Army law states that an AWOL soldier who has handed himself in cannot be detained in the jail, he is free until a court-martial is arranged.

'Report to the guardroom every night, now fuck off back to your platoon,' ranted the regimental policeman, who had been quite calm about the whole thing.

I headed straight back to my block. The room was almost empty, there were one or two new faces. Upstairs I met Craig and I started telling him everything that had happened. Enter Sergeant Read, who nearly had a fit when he saw me. He was a loner and a serious arsehole. 'Fucking stand up, you scumbag!' I did, mumbling under my breath. I could feel the tears well up in my eyes. 'You're a fucking disgrace, you wanker!' he was screaming in my face and at the same time spitting all over me. I have never felt so small in my life. 'Get fucking outside, you're going to jail.'

'I handed myself in,' I protested.

'I don't fucking give a shit – get outside.'

This nasty piece of work then doubled me to the guardroom. Meantime, I'm visualising how it would feel to kill this bastard, it would be very satisfying. Inside the guardroom, the provost corporal explained that I shouldn't be jailed, there was no reason for it.

'Just get him in the fucking cells, Corporal,' Sergeant Read said, emphasising the word 'corporal'.

'Through the back, Donnan,' ordered the provost corporal, he too was getting stroppy.

I was stripped naked and given a pair of green overalls and a hairy army blanket.

'Get in there,' he said, pointing to my cell.

As the door banged shut, I cringed. This was a sound I grew to hate and fear. At that point I realised the army were a law unto themselves, I was nothing more than a name and number, I was a nobody. The close confines of the cell soon had me pulling out my hair and I developed a real phobia about being locked up. When someone takes away your freedom, they rob you of everything.

The madness that surrounded my life never seemed to end, when would it all stop? Once more I had no control over my life. I wanted to die, right there and then, at least that way I would have no more torment. 'Typical,' I thought, 'no fucking guns when I really needed one!' Maybe I could eat the mattress, that would surely kill me, but it would take days just to eat the fucking thing. The bastards had even robbed me of the choice to kill myself. Not only was I in the army, they fucking owned me, my arse was theirs. In the morning I would have to escape, I didn't know how, but I would have to go.

At 0500 hours I was told to get washed and shaved. For the first time in weeks I looked at my gaunt face in a mirror. I didn't recognise myself, it was scary.

'Donnan!' summoned the provost corporal. I walked from the toilets through to the front desk, where the provost corporal was sitting. 'Get through the fucking back – and come in here properly, don't let me see you walking again.'

It was silly games time, at fucking five in the morning. This was the last thing I needed. Out of pure temper I sprinted all the way back towards the front desk, thinking I'll show the bastard. The guardroom floor was highly polished, in fact, it was like glass. Just as I got to the desk I slipped, I crashed to the floor and landed with a dull thud.

'Who told you to breakdance? Get fucking up!' the provost corporal said, pissing himself laughing. 'Get a brush and start cleaning up,' I was told. For the next two hours I brushed up, polished things, made tea for the duty policeman, which I pissed in. This made me feel better somehow. It evened up the score at bit. At just after seven, I was released back to my platoon pending a court-martial. I was under strict orders to report to the guardroom twice a night, also they confined me to the camp. I had other plans, I wanted to put as much distance between me and the army as possible.

After breakfast – this was the only good point – I received my final, final blow: all my army kit had been stolen, every last bit. I felt betrayed. The thieves were people I had gone to war with, people I had once trusted. From that day on I learned to trust no one.

Time for a sharp exit. I was smuggled out of camp inside a car boot. My driver, who shall remain nameless, dropped me at the local railway station. I travelled to Glasgow, dodging the ticket collector all the way. Later that night I made it back to the cold, damp squat I now called home. That night, as I lay on the floorboards, my thoughts were confused. I knew nothing, I have never felt so alone in my life, it was like drifting in space. I sat on the floor and screamed, everyone got it, God, the army and me. For me the world had stopped turning. I could see no way out, there was no future, I was stuck in the past.

Soon I was back at the local doctor, who could give me no advice, instead he handed me a piece of paper saying only: 'Take these four times a day.' It was a prescription for happy pills. He said they would make me better. They didn't work. If anything, the tablets made me worse: the nightmares seemed even more vivid, my outbursts of rage increased, often directed at totally innocent people. I felt as if people were staring at me. On more than one occasion I grabbed someone by the throat and threatened to kill them. The poor fuckers were always terrified, the tempers for me resembled those of the Incredible Hulk, one minute I was normal, next thing I was a mad, psychopathic monster. For the few minutes the attacks lasted, I had no control, it was as if I was in another dimension. The ferocity of my temper always scared me. I felt so strong, I really did believe I could kill someone with my bare hands. This was all alien to my nature as I had always been quiet and was never a fighter. So much had changed, even my personality. Maybe I turned green too, nothing seemed impossible as far as I was concerned.

If I'd had money, drink would have been my friend, but even that eluded me. Instead, I turned to running. This was my self-abuse. I would run for hours, till my body was in great pain. Sometimes I would run 20-odd miles. I enjoyed hurting myself, don't ask why.

In between all this madness the cops were still hounding me;

they never stopped knocking on the door, all day and night. They were now turning up in huge numbers, four or five cars were not uncommon, catching me was now becoming a high priority for them. Deep down in my heart I knew that one day my luck would run out. I just didn't want to think about it when getting through each day was hard enough.

It was around this time I met up with my younger sister, Aynslie, and her new boyfriend, Hugh, who was also on the run from the police. It was nothing serious, just a warrant out for unpaid fines. We all ended up living in the flat together and I was glad of the company. We had no money, no food and no life. We quickly agreed on one thing – we would have to go elsewhere and live and, hopefully, we could get some work. Our biggest problem was transport, or the lack of it.

We didn't steal the car, the police call it 'taking without the owner's consent'. Anyway, we didn't get very far. Hugh was driving and I was in the passenger seat, it was the early hours of the morning and the frost was hard on the ground.

'I can't see a fucking thing,' Hugh said, head hanging out the window, trying to see what was going on.

'It's really dark, maybe it's the frost on the windscreen,' I said, puzzled by our lack of vision.

We drove down the dark side street and turned on to the main road, still unable to see very much. Right on cue, a police patrol car passed us, flashing its headlights. We both realised at the same time that we were driving with no lights on. 'Fucking put your foot down,' I said, looking behind us.

'Where to?'

'Anywhere, just hurry up.'

The police had quite rightly become suspicious and decided to give chase. We later found out that the car we had stolen belonged to a local police officer. Just my fucking luck.

'Come on, go for it,' I said, getting impatient.

The cop car was now right behind us, with the blue lights

flashing, there was only one policeman in the car, which gave us a better chance of escape.

'Drive into the petrol station and we'll make a run for it,' I said to Hugh, who was in a state of panic. As soon as the car stopped beside the petrol pumps I was out and running. Hugh was nowhere to be seen. 'Shit!' I exclaimed to myself. I was angry, how could we have been so fucking stupid?

I gathered my thoughts and decided to head back towards the petrol station, then I could see what was going on. I checked my watch, I had just over an hour of darkness left. Parallel to the petrol station was a small wooded area where the undergrowth was a couple of feet high, it was perfect. Using all my best infantry skills, I quietly crawled towards the edge of the trees and within a couple of minutes I could see and hear everything that was taking place. I was no more than ten metres from the police, who now had Hugh in handcuffs and propped against the police car. It was a very still night, I could hear a pin drop.

'Who was in the car with you?' asked the policeman repeatedly.

'I don't know,' Hugh was saying.

The policeman checked inside the stolen car with his torch and I could see him reaching down for something. That's when I remembered my army rucksack was on the floor, worse still, it had my name and army number on it. The cop was on to it straightaway.

'Could we have the dog unit, please. We have an escaped prisoner, Barry Donnan, in the area.' I watched intently as Hugh was bundled into the police car and taken away. The dog van arrived accompanied by two other police cars. The police dog-handler then set on my trail. I reckoned I had about five minutes before the dog would come round full circle to my present position. My mind was racing, then I remembered something from my army training, if I could reach water and get in then the dog would lose my scent. I had to make for the nearby river.

After a count of three, I got up and sprinted towards the road, once across that I scrambled through the bushes towards the water. The adrenalin took over and I didn't even have to think about it, but as I hit the cold, dark water, my heart nearly stopped. I floated downstream, trying rather pathetically to swim, the bitter cold sapping any strength I had. Once I crawled out on the opposite bank, I had serious problems. I would have to cross a dual carriageway, which the police were driving up and down. At that one moment in time I had only one thought: not to get fucking caught! If that happened I'd be in deep shit, my arse wouldn't even touch the ground. The thought of a court-martial and a lengthy jail sentence terrified me, as I knew the army would be unsympathetic towards my problems. It was a good incentive as I sprinted across the road, straight into the path of an off-duty fireman who was walking to work. I don't know who got the biggest fright. He immediately sussed the police were looking for me. Like all good citizens he started jogging towards a police van some distance away. I hid in some gorse bushes though not before I watched our hero flag down the van, and point in my general direction. I dared not move, the van was right beside me, they couldn't fail to see me, I was captured for sure. Then suddenly they drove away, my luck was still in. As daylight broke, I started heading back towards the flat, continually scanning the area for cops.

'We've been caught,' I said to Aynslie, shaking her awake.

'Where is Hugh?' she asked.

'The cops have got him, I made a run for it.'

'You're joking.'

'Do I look as if I'm fucking joking?' I said, still dripping wet.

As I changed out of my wet clothing, I somehow knew the police would go all out to find me. Now I had committed a criminal offence it meant the police could apply for a warrant to search the flat.

My luck was rapidly running out and I had nowhere to turn.

Until this point in my life I had never once been in trouble with the law, or indeed anyone, and my army service record was exemplary. Once again I had no control over my life, it was a case of waiting to see what would happen next. I half-expected the police at the door that morning but, strangely, they never appeared, maybe they had forgotten all about me. I took the unusual step of cleaning myself up. I even scrounged the money for a haircut. Like I said, something told me today would be the day. I tried to be brave. Maybe this was supposed to happen, you know, fate and all that.

That evening, as I lay on the floor asleep, I heard a couple of loud bangs, followed by the sound of crunching wood. When I realised what was going on it was too late. The front door had been kicked in, the cops handcuffed me and dragged me up by the hair. I was still dressed in my running shorts and a T-shirt as they wouldn't even allow me to get changed. They gripped me tightly, in fact, four officers led me down the stairs, each one holding various parts of my body. Aynslie was behind me, screaming and crying, I was in tears and feeling sorry for myself. As I was shoved into the police car, I remember feeling like a mass murderer, or someone who would warrant the use of six police vehicles. In every part of the street was a police car. Most of the neighbours had come out to see what was going on. I hung my head in shame. At the station I was processed: mug-shots, fingerprints and a couple of interviews, all the usual bullshit.

'The army have been informed, and they are not very happy,' said the police sergeant.

'What is going to happen to me?' I asked, though deep down I really didn't want to know.

'You'll be up at court in the morning, then the army will take you back to England.'

'Please, don't let them do anything to me,' I pleaded.

'It's nothing to do with me,' he said, shaking his head, disinterested.

With that I was taken to a cell. As the door banged shut I lay down and cried. You know what was the hardest bit? No one gave a fuck. I was on my own again, me versus the whole, wide world. I didn't feel like a normal human being, it was as if I had been excommunicated from everyone. To keep my one brain cell occupied I started doing press-ups, sit-ups and jogged on the spot, anything, just don't think, keep the brain in neutral, there's less pain that way. It was not as easy as it sounds as my mind would always wander back to the army. All I could think was why? Why me? Yet fucking more questions, never any fucking answers. All I wanted was someone, anyone, to tell me it was going to be okay; that never happened. Anyway, they would have been lying, things were not okay, not then, not ever. This was torture at its best, under lock and key whilst suffering from a mental illness, an illness that I acquired serving my Queen and country. Surely that alone should stand for something? In the coming months it became apparent that it meant nothing. I was treated like a leper. My thoughts were so confused, I could see no future, I found it hard enough to get by hour to hour. As if things weren't bad enough I started to develop a form of claustrophobia.

My view of the world was through a small, heavily set window. I pressed my face against it as I needed to see outside, just to make sure this was for real. The view was disappointing, several police cars lined side by side. I turned my attention to the cell. It was disgusting, with graffiti all over the walls and a small toilet in the corner – which looked as if it hadn't been cleaned since the place was built. It had stale air about it, the walls had been painted several times, in a mushroom-brown colour, that alone was enough to make you sick. Then the door was a thick, blue, steel fucker, with a small hatch. Every now and again it would squeak open and faces would peer in. The place drove me crazy. I wanted out, now. Once more I cried, poor me, poor you, poor all of us, we were all so ignorant about life, so disinterested in the things that really matter. If you knew what I did, believe me you would feel the same way. More than anything in the world I wanted to be innocent again. I wanted to go back to being a 16-year-old with normal thoughts but, like everything else, this too was gone.

At some point, I don't remember when, I was taken from the cell and paraded around the station as the shift wanted to meet me. My ability to escape from various situations had become almost legendary within the station. After that I was hand-cuffed between two elderly tramps for my court appearance. This caused much amusement for the police. As I said earlier, at the time of my arrest I was wearing my running kit, across my charity running shirt it had the words 'Help the Aged'.

After a short journey with the drunken pensioners as companions, I was transferred to the cells below the court where I would appear later. For the first time since the incident I met Hugh. We tried to have a conversation through the steel bars but the turnkey told us to shut up. This cell was luxury compared to the first one, it had a steel toilet and toilet paper. I was gradually moving upmarket. After several hours I was hauled up in front of the local sheriff, who was furious.

'Why is this man dressed in running kit?' he asked.

'These were the clothes he was wearing at the time of arrest, your honour,' replied my lawyer.

'I see,' said the sheriff, shaking his head in disgust. That probably sealed my fate.

My lawyer explained that I was AWOL from the army and had been for some time, it was also mentioned I was suffering from PTSD. Once again no one was interested, the system didn't care, I was just another criminal in their eyes.

'The military police are waiting outside to collect Mr Donnan, your honour.' This was news to me. The thought of going back to the army filled me with absolute dread. I would rather die than go back there.

'I am unwilling to let the accused return to the army. He must be tried at this very court, therefore the accused is remanded in custody for three weeks – take him down,' the sheriff said, without even looking up from his paperwork. I was taken down into a holding cell below the court. It was filled with the dregs of society, people I had never come across in my life. I was now one of them. At least I had escaped the clutches of the army system for a while.

That afternoon I was transported to HMP Barlinnie in Glasgow which was a frightening experience. I was surrounded by murderers and rapists. Even the police seemed scared of them. I never once opened my mouth, I didn't want to upset anyone. I had enough problems without making enemies in there.

'Get in there and strip naked,' said the prison officer, pointing to a small cubicle. 'What the fuck's going to happen now?' Was this some kind of initiation ritual, getting shagged up the arse by the prison staff? I just didn't know what to expect, I'd heard many stories about life in the jail. After about five minutes we were ordered back outside the cubicles, about ten of us, standing there, bollocks swinging in the wind. 'Cough,' ordered the doctor, holding my nuts in one hand. The doctor moved along the line doing his job, and what a job it was, poor bastard. I was then thrown a set of prison clothes, which I couldn't get into quickly enough. The clothes didn't have arrows on them, as I expected, instead it was a red-striped shirt and a pair of blue denims. Looking back, I can see that the way this was carried out – making us stand there naked and stripping us of our clothes and thus our identity – was designed to humiliate us and it worked very well. I was then handed a bowl of something. This was affectionately nicknamed 'the doggie bowl' because of its resemblance to dog food. It looked disgusting and I decided I would rather starve. Then came the bit I dreaded most, being caged up, followed by the slamming of the door. I shared my cell with an average loony whose hobby was holding up petrol stations with a revolver.

'Done seven of the fuckers,' he boasted.

'Really.'

It turned out that jail was his second home. He then filled me in on the lowdown, as he put it, the unwritten rules of the prison. I wasn't really interested as I didn't intend to stay in there very long. I hoped someone would see sense and let me out. Within a short time it was lights out and an eerie silence descended on the place. I lay on top of the bed, I was scared to sleep. All I remember feeling is resentment and anger at everyone, especially my employers. It was around this time that I realised something was wrong with me, my life had changed so much, not only that, I was a different person. My life would never be the same again, my mind had been poisoned. I always ended up going back over everything in my mind, every single hour of every day: the headless, legless bodies at Lockerbie, Cloyd's bloated body as he lay dead at the door of the helicopter and the dead Iraqi soldiers lying abandoned in the sand. All I know is that I wanted to be with them, dead and peaceful, my soul was being ripped apart. It was as if the devil had crawled inside my body and was tormenting me. I wanted to cry, but the tears wouldn't come. I was numb, confusion reigned. Where would all this end? It seemed to me like a bottomless pit, falling and falling into an abyss of total madness. My surroundings only made matters worse.

As I watched from the cell window, I saw something that briefly calmed me, the rising of the sun, daylight was near. Maybe this would be the day it would all go away and I could live again. If only things had gone as planned then I would now be learning to fly Gazelle helicopters for the army. Instead, I was locked up in this shithole. My life had changed so much in a matter of months.

That morning after breakfast I was transferred to HMP Longriggend, where I would be held until the court case. On arrival, the prison officers quickly sussed that I was very unwell so they placed me on a special suicide watch, which basically meant that I was checked on every 15 minutes. Most of the prison officers were ex-squaddies, so I was well looked after. Day after day I wallowed in self-pity and soon I lost track of time; had I been in here for a hundred years, or was it a few hours? The boredom of being locked up all day took its toll. I examined every inch of that cell, every brick, every layer of cement in between, every dust particle in the place. I even thought about trying to escape, but the prison was very secure, I would have no chance. After some time had passed, several days I think, although I'm not too sure, I was summoned to see the senior prison officer, who had a pleasant surprise for me.

'You've been released on high court bail, Donnan.'

'Thank you, sir,' I said, excited at the prospect of freedom.

'The condition being that you return immediately to your regiment.'

'When, sir?'

'Today, as soon as,' he said, looking at his watch.

The thought of going back to Cambridge made me feel sick, even talking about it gave me that knotted feeling in my stomach. I would rather have stayed in here.

'When is the escort coming for me, sir?'

'There is no escort, you're travelling under your own steam. We'll give you a travel warrant. Now go and gather your kit.'

As I left his office and headed back to the cell, I was gobsmacked. The army should have arranged an escort to pick me up, after all, I had been AWOL for months, plus I had also escaped on one occasion. This was too good to be true, an opportunity not to be missed.

Within an hour I was standing outside the front gates, armed with a travel warrant and about two pounds in loose change. Being outside again was weird. The wide-open space frightened me, normal sounds like cars and buses driving past had me jumping inside, even people talking hurt my head. I didn't feel safe, but at least I was free again. Before I knew what I was doing, I had travelled back to the squat. The place was a shithole, but for some reason I felt secure in there. I vowed never to return to the British Army as I firmly believed it would be the death of me. One of my first tasks was to find out what day and month it was, I had no idea, that's how confused I was. It turned out I had been in the nick for 14 days, that was a surprise. The case was due to be heard at the court in seven days' time, but surely the army would catch me then. I had never been in a court in my life, but I imagined the place would be swarming with cops. I would just have to deal with it when the time came.

Within hours, the police visits to the flat started again, and for the millionth time in my life I hid. Once more I was an AWOL soldier, except this time it was worse. I had escaped twice and I had broken the conditions of my high court bail. The authorities desperately wanted me behind bars so they could have a quiet life. It didn't matter that I was a mentally ill soldier, it didn't matter that I had never once been in trouble before, in fact, come to think of it, fuck all mattered, least of all me and my problems. I tried hard not to be bitter, but it was nearly impossible, I could never forgive the army, not then and certainly not now. My once-beloved regiment, a regiment to which I had given my everything, now meant little or nothing to me, they had ceased to exist in my mind.

All day and night I would hide, leaving only for a short time in the early hours of the morning. For 20 minutes I would sneak about stealing milk from doorsteps – this became my staple diet, eight bottles of milk a day. Occasionally, I would come across a bottle of fresh orange juice, which was a welcome change. One morning I even found a crate of bread, but I couldn't eat any of it as it was frozen solid, just my fucking luck.

With my camouflage bag full of milk, I would then jog back to the squat, all the time looking over my shoulder for cops. Once or twice I had a few close brushes, but I always managed to escape.

Life really was pretty shit and I have no idea how I managed to survive. I had always been well motivated and strong inside and at the time these two attributes must have helped me through. But something else also helped me survive – being a coward. I wanted more than anything to be dead, but I was too scared to kill myself, I didn't have the guts. Looking back on this, I'm fucking glad as killing myself would mean the army had won, a small victory for them, another suicide that could be quietly hushed up and the true facts would never be known. No, I owed it to myself and all the others like me, some who are dead, all heroes, to stay and fight right to the bitter end, then if I still felt the same way I would kill myself. Time alone would tell.

The morning of the court appearance soon came. As I walked into the sheriff court I felt like a lamb going to the slaughter. I was literally walking into a trap, my time on the run was going to be over, but I had no other choice. Sure enough, the court was crowded with cops and other hangers-on. For the first time since the incident I met up with Hugh and Aynslie and we exchanged some stories and then headed into the court to await our fate. Twice I ran out of the court to be physically sick. The thought of going back made me ill, I didn't have the courage to face it, all that time being locked up again, the slamming of the door, the confines of those cells, the uncertainty of it all. Back in the courtroom I remembered my appearance in Belize, that day a hundred years ago, when I was last judged. Justice was only a word in my opinion, it never existed in my world, never.

The proceedings started and the procurator fiscal decided to drop the charges against me. They figured I had enough problems with the army – that was nice of them. Hugh was fined and banned from driving for 18 months. He was quite happy with the outcome.

'Excuse me, I'm Fusilier Barry Donnan and the army is supposed to be picking me up after the court case,' I said to the clerk of the court.

He shook his head and shuffled through his paperwork, mumbling something, which I couldn't hear. 'I don't know anything about it – take a seat over there and I'll get back to you,' he said, pointing to several plastic chairs. 'What is your name again?' he asked.

'Barry Donnan.'

I did as I was told and sat there for nearly two hours but no one ever got back to me. There was no mad dash or struggle for freedom, I simply walked out of the court, down the steps and went AWOL again. No one seemed to care what happened to me, it certainly looked that way from my side of things. However, my luck was rapidly running out. As I started to get weaker, my guard came down, I no longer had my wits about me. They too had gone, just like everything in my life.

That same night I became so hungry I thought I would die. I needed food there and then. I had no money and I was desperate. With this in mind I started walking the streets, scavenging for food. It was dark and so cold and I glared with envy at people sitting in their nice, warm, cosy homes, stuffing their faces. At one point, I stood and stared in a local greengrocer's window. Stacked inside were six boxes of cereal and I contemplated doing a smash-and-grab, but something stopped me. All I wanted was something to eat, anything, I wasn't fussy. I was too proud to beg, plus the streets were empty, well, almost, in the distance I could see a drunk staggering about, not only that, he was carrying something. I ran towards him for a closer look. It was a fish supper, I could smell it, in fact, I could almost taste it.

'Look, mate, I'm starving, any chance of some chips, please?' I inquired.

'Fuck off! These are for me and the wife,' he slurred, pissed out of his mind.

As I have said before, desperate times call for desperate measures and this was one of those occasions. I snatched the food parcel and ran hard, adrenalin helping me on a bit.

'Come back, you fucker, I'll fucking kill you!' he was shouting. Next time I looked round he had fallen over and was skidding along the road like Superman, still shouting: 'You dirty bastard!'

Once I was a safe distance away, I hid in some trees and started shoving the food down my throat. It tasted delicious; I had been saved by a fish. Since that day I have eaten many fish suppers but none has ever tasted as good as that one. Two days later I passed the man I had mugged, his arm was in plaster and his chin was stitched up, the poor bastard. Luckily, he never recognised me.

Back at the flat, I had some guests: my sister and her boyfriend. I was glad to see them – especially as they had a small amount of money, which allowed me to buy some decent food for a day or two. Food in my belly was a big bonus. I had now become painfully thin, my body was both physically and mentally shattered.

The following morning it happened, the moment I feared more than any other. It was my own fault. Earlier that morning I had been wandering round inside the flat, as usual I couldn't sleep. Someone knocked gently on the door, it didn't sound like the police, they were usually loud and aggressive, no, this definitely sounded different. I paused for a few seconds, unsure what to do, then the knock came again. 'Who is it?' I asked, whilst leaning towards the door.

'Strathclyde Police – open the door now!'

'Oh, fuck, here we go,' I thought. I froze to the spot, wishing I could just dissolve into the floor.

'Open the door!' came the shout. They were starting to get really impatient.

Quickly I tiptoed upstairs, trying not to make another sound. I woke up Aynslie and Hugh, who were sleeping on the floor, wrapped in an old sheet. 'Come on, get fucking up – hurry, it's the cops.' As they struggled awake, the front door was vibrating, the police were knocking hell out of it. 'Hugh, go down and tell them you haven't seen me since the court. I'll hide somewhere.'

Looking around the flat, I quickly realised my choice of places to hide was fairly limited. I could scarcely hear the conversation between Hugh and the police. I grabbed a blanket and squeezed behind a large wardrobe, where I crouched down and pulled the blanket over my head. The minutes slowly ticked away. The police were in the flat now. 'Mind if we take a look round?'

'No – look, we don't know where Barry is,' Aynslie was saying, trying her best to mislead them.

For more than ten minutes the cops searched likely hiding places. Meantime, I was behind the wardrobe, shit scared to breathe never mind move. 'Right, everything's okay, we've had a look around, if you see Barry . . .' The policeman then remembered that he hadn't checked behind the wardrobe so he pulled the wardrobe out and there I was still hiding under the blanket, trying to deny this was really happening. 'Right, you bastard, get out,' said the cop venomously, at the same time grabbing me by the hair. I was then placed in handcuffs and dragged down the stairs. I refused to walk. At one point I grabbed hold of the banister and held on for dear life. It took four police officers to prise my fingers apart and break my grip. For me it had all happened so quickly. Outside in the street were four police cars. The amount of manpower the police always used amazed me.

At the local police station I was immediately thrown into a

cell. I didn't scream, I didn't cry, I lay down on the bed and pulled the grey, hairy blanket over my head. For hours I lay there. My mind raced over my past, the bad times and the good. I felt nothing but confusion. The army was finally going to get what they wanted: me.

I didn't give a toss. Who cares? No one, that's who.

7. Marking Time

I was well pissed off, and I think I had good reason to be.

'You, sonny, are several grades lower than the shit on my shoe. Do you fucking understand?'

'Yes, Staff.'

It was humiliation time again, acting like children, playing stupid games and going around in fucking circles. I was in my fourth day of being held in the regimental guardroom and it was a nightmare. The regimental provost staff, whose job it was to look after me or, to be more precise, to make sure I didn't escape again, were all serious half-wits with pea-sized brains. The first day I arrived back, I asked to see the medical officer. This didn't go down well with my masters.

'No, you fucking can't,' I was told. 'You'll do as I fucking say. I'll tell you when you'll see the doctor, now fuck off through the back!'

The five soldiers who made up the provost section were all bastards. They were all blokes who couldn't hack life in a rifle company, real wankers. As soon as they became regimental policemen, they adopted a strange attitude, similar to that of Hitler. Their attitude towards people was really incredible and always shocking. In the guardroom were several rifles, locked on to a weapons rack and if I could have got a weapon out and stolen some ammunition then terrible things would have hap-

I would have taken great delight in shooting the fuckers
gh the head.

is may seem a bit harsh, but they took great delight in
making my miserable life even more dismal. In my state of mind
I needed medical help, not all this bullshit. I was surrounded by
the enemy, at least that's how it felt.

On my fifth day of internment I was marched to the medical
centre as the medical officer had asked to see me.

'Take a seat, Fusilier Donnan.'

'Yes, sir.'

'How are you?'

'Oh, I'm having a fucking great time, sir.'

'Really,' was all he said. Then he proceeded to stare at me for
a few moments, saying nothing. I stared back. The doctor
shifted uneasily in his seat.

'I have some medical reports here from your local GP,' he
mumbled as he quickly flicked through the paperwork. 'Do you
ever feel depressed?'

'All the time, sir. I just want to be alone.'

'Mmmmm, leave it with me. Oh – take these four times a
day,' he said, handing me a bottle of happy pills.

'Okay, sir.'

I got up and headed towards the door. When I opened it, I
wasn't surprised to find the regimental cop had been standing
with his ear against it, trying to listen in. 'Give me the tablets,'
he demanded.

Once outside the building I was doubled back to the guardroom. Years later I read what the doctor had written that day. He
stated that I suffered from PTSD and severe depression, also that
being in jail suited me, being alone and all that. I wasn't aware at
the time, but the doctor was worried enough to contact the
psychiatric department at Queen Elizabeth Military Hospital in
Woolwich to see if they would do a psychological assessment.
This never happened. Someone, somewhere, made sure of that.

For me the future looked bleak. I would be held in the guardroom until such time as a court-martial could be arranged. This could take months, then, no doubt, I would get sentenced and my punishment would be four or five months in the land of striped sunshine. Life in the guardroom was strange. I was hardly ever spoken to but if I was it was in one of two different tones of voice: one was loud and the other even louder. I was officially classed as a SAT (soldier awaiting trial) so everyone treated me like a scumball. Not once did anyone ask why I had gone AWOL. They didn't want to know the circumstances, all they wanted was to put me through a court-martial, then I would get what I justly deserved.

Every day I popped my little happy pills, my treatment in a bottle. They had very little effect on me. Give them their due, though, they did calm me down slightly and without them I would have killed someone in the guardroom. This place was how I imagined hell to be, stuck in here forever, listening to the droll conversations of those narrow-minded, nasty, horrible little shits. I have often wondered how those guys could live with themselves. Did they have a conscience? I honestly don't think so. Maybe that's something that happens after years in the army.

Next day, it was more bad news: I was to be court-martialled in two weeks' time. The regiment wanted me back at work quickly, hence the hastily organised trial. The adjutant informed me that I should decide on a defending officer quickly. At a push, I could have a civilian lawyer to defend me, but that wasn't recommended. Under pressure, I elected to choose a relatively new and junior subaltern from my regiment. Looking back, it was a big mistake. However, my defending officer, Lieutenant Andrews, was a good and honest man, one of only a few. Preparations for the impending court-martial started that same day. I was marched to the QM's department to be reissued with full army kit to replace everything that had been nicked. I was billed for nearly £1,000. In the afternoon, Lt Anderson came to visit me in the cells. We discussed my best form of defence and how he would best use it. He reckoned I would be punished lightly as the mitigating circumstances were very strong and the fact that I had been such a good soldier would definitely help my case.

'Don't worry about a thing,' he told me, leaving the cell.

'Thanks, sir.'

This was some good news. Maybe everything would work out fine and then I could finally leave the army and put this mess behind me forever. My defending officer and I had something in common: we were both naive. Stupidly, we both believed in the big system.

The drudgery of life in the guardroom was really getting me down. I was just managing to hold on and no more. A typical day would be up at 0500 hours, when I was given ten minutes to have a wash and shave. For the next hour and a half before breakfast it was chore time: sweeping, brushing and shining floors. During this mind-numbing task you would always get a bollocking – usually for something trivial. Then it would be outside for the physically exhausting march to the cookhouse. Once inside the building, I was under strict rules: no speaking, no smiling and I was always kept away from everyone else. I would then be given about three minutes to eat my scoff and get back outside. 'By the front, double march! Left, right, left, right!' the duty policeman would shout. After ramming a scoff down your throat, the speed marching was a nightmare. I got stomach cramp every time.

'Mark time!'

I would stop marching forward, instead it was like jogging on the spot, except harder. My feet had to strike the ground as he called out the pace.

'Left, right, left, right, left – get your fucking legs moving, you idle fucker! Forward.'

Then I would move off again, arms swinging shoulder high,

neck in the back of the collar and chest out, like some pathetic pigeon.

'Get your shagging arms up, toad, or I'll stick this cane through your ears and drive you about the camp like a fucking motorbike.'

All this shit at seven o'clock in the morning definitely wasn't good for you. Back in the guardroom it would be cleaning time again. In between this you would make tea for any fucker who wandered into the building and was thirsty. This was something I always enjoyed, especially putting things in their tea and, depending on how much I hated them and the amount and type of flotsam I could find, these ranged from piss and snot to insects. I watched and laughed in amazement one day as I witnessed a fellow prisoner stir the RSM's tea with his cock.

You may think this is sick but at the time we were strange people living under bizarre rules. All day I would be kept busy. If I was really lucky then I would be sent outside with an escort and, armed only with a brush, I would spend hours sweeping up leaves. Twice a day my kit would also be inspected by the duty officer, who would ask if I had any complaints. This was my chance to voice any opinions – of course, I said nothing. Late evening was a time of inactivity but, to keep me occupied, the adjutant or the RSM would hand in various pieces of their kit, usually boots and sometimes a sword, to polish. At around midnight I could lie on my bed, then the door would be slammed shut and locked. Cold and alone, I would search every corner of my soul, trying to grasp for any hope I had left in my life. I could think of very little.

One day all this will end and then I'll be happy, I would often tell myself. Funny that, nearly eight years on and I'm still telling myself the same thing, still waiting for all the pain to go but I doubt it ever will. Then I would get really angry at the injustice of it all. Let me tell you something, people who suffer from PTSD should not be locked up. Being alone in a cell and suffering from flashbacks and nightmares, it doesn't help very much, in fact, I would say it's a form of mental torture.

For me, time passed in a haze of bullshit, cleaning and being shouted at. Every day was the same as the one before and this alone was soul-destroying stuff. The next major drama was caused by the medical officer (MO) just two days before my court-martial. I had a strict medical, which is normal procedure – basically, it's just a formality to check if you're fit to stand trial. After a quick check over, the doctor told me to take a seat which I did, while he flicked through my notes, which seemed to be growing daily.

'I don't think you're fit enough to go through a court-martial, in fact, I don't think you should even be in detention at all,' said the MO, who appeared genuinely concerned.

'So, what now, sir?' I asked hopefully.

'I'll have to speak with the commanding officer before any decisions can be made,' he replied.

'Okay, sir.'

'Good luck,' was all he said as I got up to leave.

As I was marched back to the guardroom, I became even more confused. The doctor was saying I was unfit for detention, yet they were still holding me in the jail. Surely they wouldn't proceed with a court-martial against the doctor's orders, that would be criminal. More to the point, it would be downright negligent. In my time I'd heard a few horror stories, mainly about the army failing people in times of distress. I knew they could stoop low, but they had rules. No, I gave them the benefit of the doubt, someone would see sense. I was to learn much later on something very important: army doctors have the power to overrule even the commanding officer, who was a lieutenant-colonel. The conversation between me and the doctor resulted in absolutely nothing; that's all it was, a conversation, a crock of shit.

The day before the court-martial was spent preparing my best uniform; it had to be immaculate. I had ironed my kit three or four times as I didn't want to give anyone an excuse to give me yet another bollocking. Lieutenant Anderson came to see me in the afternoon and he assured me that everything was under control and that I didn't have to worry. He also reckoned I would get a sentence of about four weeks, tops. Guess what? I really believed him. He seemed so confident and positive about the situation, I thought he must have had inside information, plus that's the way we are trained, officers lead and we follow without asking questions. My company sergeant-major also paid me a visit but not to give any comfort, just a hard time.

'You are a fucking wanker, Donnan. You were going places at one time, before you became a waster – I hope they throw the book at you,' he growled at me under his moustache as he held his pace stick up my nostrils. For the very first time ever in my army career, I thought about punching a senior rank but somehow I managed to stay calm. 'Take your punishment like a man, Donnan,' said the sergeant-major before leaving the cell.

After he had been gone a few seconds I punched the wall and thought of the sergeant-major's twisted face. I wanted to kill the narrow-minded bastard.

At midnight the duty policeman gave my kit a final once over, after he had approved it with a nod he told me to get some sleep. I lay down on the bed and sighed. I had no energy, no interest. My new method of dealing with the madness that surrounded my life was to switch off. It was like being a child again, pretending, living in a self-created fantasy world. It was the only course of action I could take. This was the denial stage. I remember feeling a strange sort of nothingness. I wanted to feel something but, no matter how hard I tried, I simply couldn't. Sleep followed in short bursts. I would bounce awake every 20 minutes or so and so it was a long, hellish night. At 0500 hours I was gently awakened by someone shouting.

'Right, fucking time to get up and face the music,' bellowed the provost corporal.

I felt half dead, I probably was, come to think of it. After a quick wash and shave, it was breakfast time, but I wasn't allowed near the cookhouse, so they arranged to bring the scoff to me. As I sat in the cell munching away, the padre appeared to give me some words of comfort. It felt as if I were eating my last supper and soon they would take me out the back and shoot me, just like they had done in the First World War. Between 1914 and 1918, 306 soldiers were executed for cowardice, many of whom were known to have suffered shell-shock. Brave men were shot at dawn by firing parties from their own regiments. Sick or what? I don't know about you, but things like that gave me an uneasy feeling in my stomach. The government talked about giving them a pardon, but they shouldn't have to talk about it, it should have been done, yesterday. I think many of my regiment would probably have liked to see me shot at dawn – just for the sake of example.

Eventually, after plenty of fucking about, I was led outside to a waiting minibus. Two minders were on either side of me to make sure I didn't do a runner. I did think about escaping, but I figured it was too late for that. Anyway, it would only make matters worse – if that was possible. We travelled to London in complete silence. I was in no mood for small talk, especially with the two members of the provost staff, who were also on board. They were treating the whole thing as a day out.

After nearly two hours we arrived at Regent Park Barracks with an hour to spare before the court-martial began. I checked every inch of my uniform again, then I started to get really nervous. The surroundings were so formal and I couldn't believe that I was actually about to be court-martialled. I had always tried to be a good infantry soldier, I gave the army everything I had, 100 per cent always, never anything less but it hadn't been enough. I sat alone in a daze.

'Right, Donnan, stand up,' ordered my escort.

It was time to go and be judged. At exactly 1100 hours on 7

November 1991, I was double marched into the court.

'Are you 24823178 Fusilier Barry Donnan of the 1st Battalion the Royal Highland Fusiliers?'

'Yes, sir,' I snapped.

'You are charged with absence without leave, contrary to section 38a of the Army Act 1955, in that you did, at Oakington Barracks, Cambridge, absent yourself without leave from the 8 May till 21 October 1991,' said the president of the proceedings, who was an army major. 'How does the accused plead?'

'Guilty, sir,' said my defending officer. I just stood there, at attention, and wondered where my life would go from here.

For those of you who have never experienced a court-martial, it's just like the high court with its pompous and outdated traditions. Later, in 1997, the European Court of Human Rights ruled that the British court-martial system was illegal, but that was too late to help me.

The court-martial was made up of three officers, one major and two captains, all drawn from normal infantry regiments – in fact, one of them was from the Territorial Army. None of them was trained in law.

My adjutant then stood up, acting for the prosecution, gave a long statement of evidence and finished by saying: 'It is the commanding officer's opinion that Fusilier Donnan is a capable and well-motivated soldier whose recent behaviour has been out of character. The CO wishes to retain Donnan in the unit.'

Call me Mr Silly, but I thought that the fact they'd mentioned my strange behaviour would prove things weren't right and that I was ill. Next to speak was my defending officer. He started reading aloud my plea of mitigation. That was probably the proudest moment of my life, listening to my glittering career being read by someone else. I sounded so good, I could hardly believe it was me.

'The accused's ability as a soldier has consistently been recognised by his superiors. His application for a place on Operation Raleigh was happily endorsed by his company commander, and such was the ability of the accused that he was subsequently recommended for officer training. During the Gulf War he was employed as the company motorcycle dispatch rider, a position of responsibility for which he was selected by the company sergeant-major for reasons of his maturity and professionalism. As in all other positions that the accused has held, he has carried out his duties with a noticeably keen and conscientious attitude. Three particular events during his career have left lasting impressions upon Fusilier Donnan: his experience at Lockerbie, the death of a Belizean soldier during a foot patrol, and the subsequent inquiry, and, finally, his experiences in the Gulf. The general atmosphere, the air of expectancy and the controlled build up of aggression in the days prior to the ground war, left him feeling somewhat anti-social and at odds with himself and his friends on return to the UK. It was this that resulted in him failing to return to the battalion at the end of his disembarkation leave. Appreciating that he was undergoing a change in personality and suffering from increasing nightmares, the accused made an appointment with his local GP and was referred to a psychiatrist, a copy of whose statement is submitted in the abstract of evidence. The accused genuinely apologises for the inconvenience he has caused to the army and is truly sorry about the matter.'

I nearly collapsed when I heard him reading the last bit, the part about being sorry. Me having to apologise to those fuckers? What about all the inconvenience I had suffered? Who was going to apologise for all the nightmares and all my intrusive thoughts?

I was then marched out of the court while the powers that be decided on my future.

'Thanks for your help, sir,' I told Lieutenant Anderson, who had defended me vigorously.

'No problem. Look, don't worry, everything is going fine.'

'I hope so, sir.'

'You'll be lucky if you get 28 days.'

During a conversation with another soldier, I learned that the court-martial also had the power to dismiss me from the army. 'Yes, please,' I thought. For 20 long minutes I waited nervously, then came the order: 'By the front, double march!'

I marched into the court and halted in front of the three officers, who all looked really bored.

'24823178 Fusilier Barry Donnan, you are sentenced to 112 days' detention and soldier on.'

I didn't flinch, I was too shocked for that. I could hardly believe it, they had obviously not listened to a word that was said.

'Soldier under sentence, march out!' screamed the escort, his voice echoing round the room.

I about-turned and marched from the court, totally humiliated. I felt like running back in and saying: 'Look, you've made a big mistake,' but I didn't. The system had let me down, there was no justice in court that day. My court-martial effectively ignored an illness that was recognised even in the First World War. Everything I had struggled through counted for nothing. That made me sad and angry; my life was wasted. The court-martial had behaved irrationally, they also behaved to the point of criminal negligence. I walked from the building broken into tiny pieces. I just remember feeling so old and so tired and I had this strange feeling: I just wanted to lie down and be alone, everyone could fuck off and leave me. The strength I needed in order to fight was ebbing away. I was rapidly losing the will to live.

I was taken back to Cambridge under escort, where I would spend the night, then I would be handed over to MCTC (military correction training centre) in Colchester. This was the notorious 'glasshouse' that was so feared within the forces, and quite rightly so. As a military prisoner you surrender all your basic rights and are entitled to fuck all, no pay and half rations. The only thing you are still allowed to do is breathe, and that is about it. I was facing 112 days of incarceration. Justice, clemency, mercy – all fucking bullshit. Why did this always happen to me? Maybe I was a bad person. All this punishment, no one deserved to be treated like this. Life for me was so completely and utterly mental, it had lost control. Where would it go from here? I mean, it couldn't really get any worse. But it did, and when it got bad it was a living hell.

That final night in Cambridge I had a stream of visitors, most only wanted to gloat, or to say, 'I told you so.' Only Lieutenant Anderson seemed really upset.

'I'm really sorry,' he said, at the same time shaking my hand.

'It's not your fault, sir.'

'It never turned out as I expected.'

'Same as.'

'Good luck, Donnan, keep in touch with me.'

'Yes, sir.'

In all my time and troubles, he was the only one who really cared; that was the last time I saw him. I later learned that he blamed himself over my imprisonment for a long time. At least I wasn't the only one who was shocked at army justice.

Next morning I was transported to MCTC, just outside Colchester, which would be my home for the next couple of months. As I marched in the front gatehouse, struggling with all my kit, a voice boomed from inside the small building.

'March on to the red spot and look up!'

I checked the ground for the red mark then I lunged forward and stood on it. It was a large red circle, maybe three feet in diameter.

'Don't fucking move!'

I stood still. I was crapping myself. The voice was fearsome.

'Name?' I was asked.

'Donnan, sir.'

'Don't fucking call me sir – I work for a living. Call me Staff!'

'Typical,' I thought, 'trust me to come here when the biggest gobshite in the world was on duty.' But it turned out they were all like that. This was my introduction to the men of the Military Provost Staff Corps who ran the place. My first impression was of how hard and mean they sounded but voices can be deceptive.

After standing on the spot for 15 minutes, without moving an inch, the man behind the voice appeared. He was the skinniest, shortest man I had ever come across in army uniform, probably about the same size as Ronnie Corbett. I bit down hard on my tongue, I wanted to laugh at this mentally deranged pygmy.

'Right, listen in Donnan, go to the pace I call out, by the front, quick march!'

His voice was so fast I couldn't distinguish between left and right. It was as if he was speaking another language made up of grunts and groans. So, for my troubles, he beasted me round the camp, at 180 paces a minute, for half an hour. I had been in the place only 15 minutes and already I had made an enemy.

After my drill lesson, I was taken to the main building. The camp was divided into three holding areas: A wing for prisoners who were staying in the army, D wing for prisoners who would be booted out upon completion of sentence and then you had the block for all the high-risk prisoners – the murderers, rapists and other violent offenders. Little was known about the block, except it was a place you didn't want to go, it was the next level of hell within hell, if you like. Even looking at the small building with no windows sent shivers up my spine. Little did I know that in just over 12 months' time, I, too, would be a prisoner in there.

Once all my kit was searched and I was given the usual spiel about working hard and don't fuck us about and we'll not fuck you about, I was shown to my room. I was placed in the safe custody area with five others. I would stay here until my sentence had been confirmed by the brigadier. The building was very modern and it looked more like a small primary school inside, but a lot more secure; only two people had ever escaped. Immediately I set about unpacking my kit. Each of us had a small locker above our bed space and in it we had to place three shirts, PT kit, socks and gloves, all neatly boxed off. On our beds we placed our knife, fork and spoon in between a bed card (which had written on it your name, date of birth, regiment, religion, army number and duration of your sentence) and a cup. Everything had to be perfect, nothing was allowed to be even an inch out.

The best word to describe MCTC is bullshit. The place thrives on it, just about everything you do is meaningless, but I suppose that is the whole point of it. So I spent my first day behind an iron and I quickly learned that having neatly pressed kit was the key to success in MCTC. I became a true professional overnight.

'Get on parade!' came the shout. This was our cue to scramble out into the main corridor and form into three ranks, and bloody fast. We had to march everywhere at the double, even inside the building. Once a roll-call was made we were marched to the cookhouse. We had strict rules for mealtime – no talking, no smiling and no passing food to your neighbour; if you were caught doing any of these it could earn you an extra three days on your sentence, so it simply wasn't worth the risk. The food was crap. As prisoners we were entitled to only half-rations, so we always seemed to be hungry. After dinner it was back to the wing, then we had an hour to sort out our kit. As we had one iron between five of us, we had to be quick. At six o'clock every night we were locked up and our job then was to shine things, like boots, belts and every fixture in the room. It was hard work.

Every now and again one of the staff would peer through the

flap in the door, and God help anyone who was sitting idle. As we were working we would all sit and chat, everyone had a story to tell, we all seemed to be in for the same thing: going walkies from the army – which tells you something. At ten o'clock it was lights out, time to sleep for some, though not this soldier. I would lie awake staring at the ceiling, wondering how much more I could take. Everything was just bubbling away under the surface, like a volcano waiting to erupt. I didn't think of the future any more, as there was no point, there wasn't one. Each day was an achievement, a battle just to get from morning to night. I was a state of nothingness, nothing mattered, I had no interest in other people, I didn't care what was going on around me, the only thing I was interested in was me. This may sound selfish, but I was so wrapped up in trying to get myself through this that everything else was on the sidelines. Once or twice a night I would jolt awake, frightened out of my skull. Often I would wake up to find I'd been crying in my sleep. My mind was full of terrible thoughts, all locked away in some dusty corner of my brain but coming out to play at night.

Morning time in the glasshouse was a period of intense activity. There was so much to be done, so little time to do it. First thing was to wash and shave, followed by building a bedblock. There was an art to it: two blankets were folded then quartered and in between these you placed two bedsheets – which had to be equal width and length – this bundle was then placed on to another blanket, then you would wrap it up, taking care to keep it nice and tight, then it was put at the top of the bed. Next thing, it was cleaning out the room, brushing the floor, polishing it and checking for dust. After that it was breakfast time, all 15 minutes of it, with the crap food literally thrown down your neck. It was then another round of cleaning time and doing last-minute checks on your personal kit before the morning inspection. At exactly five minutes before eight, you stood by your bed and waited.

'Room . . . room, 'shun!'

We all snapped to attention as the duty NCO entered the room. He would slowly work his way around, checking everywhere, looking for the slightest bit of dirt or dust. Then it was our turn, as the NCO stood in front of us as we ran off our spiel: 'Staff, I am 759 Donnan, sentenced to 112 days' detention, EPDR [earliest possible day of release] 12 January 1992, Staff!'

Our uniform and bed layout would then be scrutinised, any comments, good or bad, would then be written down by the inspecting officer. If your turnout was exceptional, you would then be awarded a recommend, with six of these you would progress to stage two. Which basically meant an easier life and more responsibility, with a few perks thrown in, such as a TV room and real newspapers to read and, most importantly, you were no longer locked up at night, the door was left wide open. I made it my resolution to get there as quickly as possible.

After the inspection it was training time. For the first three weeks it was drill and PT all day long. It was a real fucking ballbreaker and you were treated like scum. It was harder than anything I have ever done before and the pressure was incredible, but I managed to hang in there. My long running stints when I had been AWOL were helping me and I was the fittest soldier in Colchester at that time. At the end of each run, the PT instructor and I were always well up front and the two of us would then race each other to the finish, the results were mixed – it just depended on who was feeling stronger that day. On one occasion I broke a long-standing record for the three-mile CFT (combat fitness test). I knocked almost 30 seconds off the old time and my instructor was delighted. I might have been fucked up in the head, but I was still a good soldier – sometimes.

Within 21 days I moved up to stage two. As this was the quickest it could be done, I was pretty pleased with myself. Troubles aside, life in Colchester wasn't that bad; if it was under

different circumstances it could have been quite
After the initial three-week breaking-in period, the
off, as long as you worked hard and kept your mouth ...
shut. I actually felt safe in Colchester, away from my regiment;
though night was always the worst time, always was, always will
be. What else was there, I had to soldier on. I checked the
dictionary for the definition of 'soldier on'. It says: 'To persist in
one's efforts in spite of difficulties, pressure etc.' That's exactly
fucking it, I was a human robot, persisting all day, every day,
trying to survive. While the whole world was going about its
business, I was locked in a military prison, fighting for
something. At the time I didn't know what it was, I do now – I
was fighting for me and my pathetic life.

As the weeks passed, the training intensified. I was learning
first aid, fieldcraft and weapon training – all to advanced levels.
Most of the training was bullshit, as by this stage I was quite an
experienced infantryman, so I knew what I was talking about.

Day after day it was the same laborious routine: up at the
crack of dawn, train all day, get shouted at, clean things, shine
things and then back to bed – no rest for the wicked. The staff
always reminded us that we were there to be punished, we had
wronged the army and this was our pay back. As if the
punishment wasn't bad enough, all our wages had also stopped
and we were skint prisoners. Even worse, if you signed on for,
say, three years and during that time you ended up in the
glasshouse, maybe doing a six-month sentence, the army could
add the six months on to the end of your contract, meaning you
would end up doing three and a half years. The bastards had us
by the short and curlies every fucking time. One thing was sure,
the army always got its money's worth, whatever the cost. Mind
you, our employer was HM Queen and Son, and they could do
what they wanted, couldn't they? It certainly seemed that way
from where I was sitting.

After being in detention for 75 days I was released back to my regiment. My report from MCTC was a good one and, through hard work, I had earned the maximum remission on my sentence. It was a place I never wanted to visit again. Only 6 per cent of prisoners reoffend after serving time in Colchester, the system works well for some. In time I would be one of those 6 per cent.

Back at Oakington Barracks, life was generally the same. The regiment was taking its turn at Spearhead Battalion, which was basically 24-hour stand-by. That meant that we would be the first unit to be deployed in the highly unlikely event of a crisis. Nothing ever happened, and it was actually a pain in the arse. Everyone was dressed in combats and carrying weapons and no one was allowed to leave the camp. Mind you, it was only for a month. I was in the camp an hour when the message came to go and see the commanding officer.

'Come in, Donnan,' he said cheerfully. I walked over and halted. 'How was Colchester?'

'It was fine, sir,' I lied. 'Sir, I want out of the army, right away,' I said rather abruptly.

'No, you can't – take ten days' leave as you missed Christmas and New Year.'

'Thank you, sir.'

'Come and see me when you get back.'

For a few hours, as I travelled home, I felt something strange, a sort of happiness. I had managed to survive Colchester and now I was a free man travelling back home to my family. There was only one problem to sort out – getting out of the British Army, alive. Things seemed to be going well, which was a rare occurrence in my messy life, when things go well, breathe deeply and enjoy it, something will always come along and fuck it right up.

As soon as I stepped into the house I knew something was wrong. My mother was in tears as she handed me a piece of paper. On it was a phone number which I recognised straightaway – it was the guardroom at Oakington. I thought that they were checking up on me already, and I wasn't very fucking happy, I'd been in the house only two minutes and they were already making demands on me. Very reluctantly I picked up the phone and dialled the number, eager to find out what was expected of me next. It had better be good, I was on my own time.

'Hello, guardroom, 1 RHF. Corporal Howard speaking, sir,' said the voice.

'Hello, it's Fusilier Donnan speaking, I've been given a message to phone.'

'Aye, get your arse back here, we're going to Northern Ireland.'

'But I'm on leave,' I protested.

'Your leave is cancelled. If you don't come back you'll be charged with desertion,' he warned.

'When do I have to report back?'

'Tonight.'

I hung up. The army had played a few blinders in its time, but this was outrageous. Within five minutes I was saying my goodbyes. My family were devastated, they couldn't understand it. Mind you, neither could I.

A couple of hours later I was in trouble. I had missed the last train to London and I was stuck in Edinburgh for the night, with no money and nowhere to sleep. It was a freezing cold January night, I was so tired, so fed up, and for the first time in ages I cried. How much more could I take? I walked out of the station and into a park. The frost lay hard on the ground. I chose a spot between some bushes and lay down. As I closed my eyes I thought of the army, they had finally broken my spirit, life held nothing for me, a strange emptiness filled me. I was alone, I always would be. At the end of the day it was just me and my troubles, nothing or no one could ever help me. My body was shivering with the cold, but I didn't feel it, I wanted to sleep, I needed to rest. Goodnight.

As I drifted away, I prayed that I would never wake up and that God would take my misery from me. I was ready to quit, I was so tired of hitting walls. For six hours I waited on death, but fuck all happened, except I shivered too much, self-induced torture. I still wanted to be dead, however, I knew it would happen soon, my days were numbered on this wretched planet. With that in mind I set out on the journey back to Cambridge, a journey that would ultimately finish off me and my career as a soldier. I would be taken to the brink, then pushed off, alone.

8. Ireland

When I reached Oakington all was not well. The company commander gave me a sound bollocking. I should have returned hours ago, he said. 'If you only knew, you bastard,' I thought. What happened next was the most controversial point in my career: the fucking army sent me to patrol the streets of Northern Ireland – which wasn't a crime, but the circumstances were. No soldier is allowed on patrol unless they have completed a certain training course, which lasts two weeks, that is a fact. While the RHF were doing the course, I was marking time in MCTC, so I was unqualified for starters, plus I was fucking mental at the time. Imagine giving someone a gun in that state, let alone ordering them to patrol the streets of Ireland. But that's what happened. I was sent to Ireland armed, untrained and mentally unwell; it was not a very wise combination. When I pointed this out to the CO I was told to 'shut up and go away'.

I should have surrendered my rifle and told them to fuck off, but I was too scared, I had already experienced jail and how they could lock you away when you hadn't really done anything wrong. I didn't want to go back there. The army could make and break their own rules, as and when they pleased.

The army had me skating over thin ice. Imagine the repercussions if I'd actually shot someone, it didn't bear thinking about. I was a danger to everyone, every soldier, every civilian and to myself.

Within 48 hours of completing a 75-day sentence, I was sitting on the tail ramp of a Chinook helicopter, staring down at the Irish countryside below. Our destination was Portadown. Our task was to start mobile Land Rover patrols, not that I was interested. The helicopter started its descent to the drop-off point, weaving hard left and right. It was tactical flying to avoid becoming a target. Mind you, once we stepped from the chopper, we were the target, walking bullet-catchers. As the heli touched down I was first out and I sprinted a short distance and took cover in a hedgerow. The noise of the Chinook was deafening and for a few minutes confusion reigned. The army barracks lay behind me, well, I presumed that was the camp, all I could see was a huge, grey blast wall. I stared down the sights of a rifle, scanning the area for movement, as the Chinook lifted into the air. Silence came quickly, but after being inside the helicopter for so long it took a couple of minutes to adjust.

'Prepare to move,' shouted my section commander. I crawled forward on my belly and moved across to my left. I had to break cover from a different position than I had entered as the enemy could have a sniper rifle trained on me and this was a ploy to fool them – that's the theory, anyway. 'Move!' I was up and running, zig-zagging all the way, soon I was in the safety of camp.

'Right, everyone gather round and I'll take you to the accommodation,' said our guide.

He needn't have bothered; 70 of us were crammed into a small drill hall where we would be sleeping on camp-beds. The shithouse was a Portakabin outside, which stank to high heaven, health and safety officials would have had a field day.

'It's not exactly the fucking Hilton, is it?' someone moaned.

'Stop complaining and get your fucking kit sorted out,' said Sergeant Roberts, who we all loathed. I groaned inwardly. Why was the man such a prick? 'Make sure this place is fucking kept clean,' he was ranting. We all looked at each other. I let out a large yawn. 'Am I fucking boring you, Donnan?'

'No, Sergeant.'

'Well, stop fucking yawning then.'

'Yes, Sergeant.'

'I'll get a list of block jobs drawn up.'

That was his mentality, two minutes in the place and he was working out cleaning rotas, it didn't matter that we were the ones living there, he could fuck off to the sergeants' mess, with all the other nobs whenever he wanted to.

'Outside in ten minutes,' came the next order.

Quickly I claimed a bed space and sorted out my kit, as we had been told. This entailed laying a sleeping bag on the camp-bed, which took about 30 seconds, hardly a big deal. Life really was pretty crap, my head was so far up my arse I didn't know what I was doing and, more to the point, I didn't really care that much. It had been almost a year since my doctor first diagnosed PTSD and still it was untreated. I just kept going, on and on, towards the path of self-destruction. I was a walking, talking, human time-bomb.

After ten minutes we traipsed out into the cold air and waited as usual. After ten minutes or so, the company commander appeared, he then gave us a short talk on our new role and told us that he expected great things from us. 'Any questions?' There was a long silence.

'When are we going home, sir?'

'I don't know. Anyway, stop asking stupid questions.'

We had been there only an hour and already blokes wanted to know about returning home, that's how rough conditions were. The place was a shithole – and that was saying something. I had become a bit of an authority on shitholes, Barlinnie, Longrigg-end, the squat and now this place.

The boss then split us into small groups and we took part in some lectures, 30 minutes on each subject, ranging from changing wheels on Land Rovers to contact drills and rules of engagement – when to shoot and when not to. All this stuff was new to me and I didn't have a clue, mind you, who did? I was a soldier taking part in a conflict that I knew fuck all about, me and half the fucking British Army. Who was the enemy? We didn't know most of the time. I had two enemies: the first was me and the second was the army. Why were they putting me through this? Because they could and they did, that's why.

We soon buckled down to the harsh realities of Northern Ireland. The hours were long and boring and 18-hour days were not uncommon. Another thing was the money was crap. Considering what you're doing – £800 a month, and all the shit you can handle, was not great recompense.

Those first few days were spent doing top cover. That meant that two of us were poking our torsos out of the Land Rover with our rifles at ready. Two highly trained soldiers, switched on and scanning the area. Bollocks! More like two freezing-cold soldiers, tired to the point of exhaustion, mostly bored out of their skulls, whose only thought is of when they would be warm again. The only time we spoke to each other was to complain about the cold.

'I'm fucking freezing.'

'Me too.'

'I'm fucking knackered.'

'Me too.'

That's about as lively as it got. We loved a good moan, and why not? There was plenty to moan about. We drove around Portadown hundreds of times a day, showing our presence and intimidating people. Occasionally, when things got really boring, we would stop and set up a snap VCP (vehicle checkpoint), randomly pulling in cars, asking them all the same questions: Where have you been? Where are you going? Mind if I search the boot? We were looking for anything suspicious, such as bombs and weapons, but we never found any. After the patrol was over, we could get some sleep, or at least try to. With so many of us in the one room it was nearly impossible as there were always people wandering about. Most of the time we would end up sleeping with our kit on, so you would lie on the bed dressed in full combats, flak jacket underneath, and boots on, helmet and rifle just ready to lift. It wasn't a very comfortable night. The trick was to pull the sleeping bag right up over your head and then you could retreat into your own small world.

In the morning, it was a quick breakfast and back out on the ground to freeze your nuts off. It was so cold that the front of our jackets would freeze solid and the visors on our helmets sometimes had a layer of thin ice covering them. I have never been so cold and tired in my life. Late at night, if things were quiet, we would drive somewhere out of the way and park up. While one soldier would stay awake and do sentry the others got some heat and, occasionally, a quick sleep.

After ten days in Portadown we were on the move to Dungannon. The living conditions were even worse: triple bunk beds, which didn't feel safe at all – the top bunk was the worst, it swayed from side to side like a hammock. It was pretty unhygienic – one of the blokes spied a rat sneaking about – and there were no recreational facilities. Fights between the soldiers were not uncommon and then usually over something trivial. It was just a way of letting off steam.

The shifts at Dungannon were just as long and hard as before, but a bit more exciting. Most of the patrol insertion and extraction was done by helicopter, which was always good for a change. The aircrew liked showing off and posing, and often they would put the chopper through its paces while we were on board. They were good pilots, though, very professional.

A typical day patrol in Dungannon was up at 0315 hours, after a wash and scoff, we would then have an intelligence briefing, about 30 minutes of information relating to such things as terrain, any trouble spots in the area and any players we could expect to encounter – known members of the IRA and other terrorist organisations. At 0500 hours we would then head out to the helipad and board the waiting helicopter, then, after a short flight, we would be dumped somewhere cold and wet. The terrain was often gruelling countryside. Hour after hour we trudged across fields, over fences, through hedgerows and ditches. On one occasion I was so bored I decided to count the number of fences we crossed, there were 200 of the fuckers in one day, most of them made of barbed wire. As we climbed over these fences we had to do it quickly and quietly, being professionals and all that, but it never worked that way. People fell flat on their faces, bits of kit got caught in the barbs and someone even managed to get their bollocks caught on the fence. Our priority was to keep moving as we didn't want to become sitting ducks. All the time you were continually scanning the area, looking over your shoulder as gunmen could be hiding almost anywhere. The pressure was pretty intense in these demanding times, and it was made harder for me because I was mentally ill. Physically, I was a wreck. I became very jumpy, with the slightest unexpected noise startling me. My temper was volatile as the contents of my head were in tatters. On the outside I looked like a normal soldier, on the inside I was crippled. For the first time in my career I began to resent the very uniform I wore, in fact actually wearing it pissed me right off. Everything was eating away at my mind, especially anger and guilt. I couldn't relax at all, it had been months since I'd had any time off and I didn't know whether I was coming or going.

After a long day on patrol we would head to the pick-up point and wait for the helicopter which was always late. This just multiplied the ever-present fuck-about factor. We would wait in the cold night air, thinking about food and heat.

'Fuck this shit, I'm buying myself out when we get back,' said Andy, the patrol second in command.

'You can't – the CO is stopping all PVRs (premature voluntary release) until June,' the platoon commander said.

'Are you joking, sir?' I asked.

'No, we're going to Canada in June. We need the bodies.'

This news shocked me. PVR was my only hope of getting out, now it seemed as if I'd be stuck in the army forever. I couldn't face that, I would have to get out soon or I'd be dead.

On the helicopter back to camp I became really depressed, I felt suffocated by the army, I just couldn't go on. It was that simple, but, as usual, things in my life were never that straightforward.

After several days in Dungannon, we moved yet again, our new home was Long Kesh, which was within the boundary of HMP Maze, a lovely place. Our new patrol areas were the east side of Belfast City. My platoon operated out of Donegal Pass RUC Station, this was later bombed by the IRA some three days after we had left. Luck was on my side for a change.

The long hours continued for the remaining month. When the tour finished, if you include my jail time, I had worked without a single day off for 25 weeks. No wonder I was done in. On 21 March 1992, we handed over to the Argyll and Sutherland Highlanders. We were going home with the regiment all in one piece. For me the tour had been uneventful, but my stress didn't go away.

Nine hours later we were safely back in Oakington Barracks. That morning I tracked down my company commander and told him that I needed out of the army, and soon.

'No,' I was told. 'Not until after June,' he said.

I started preparing for my disembarkation leave, this time I packed every bit of kit I owned, just in case it got nicked. As I was leaving the building I met my platoon commander.

'Have a nice leave, Donnan.'

'You too, sir.'

'That's an awful big bag you've packed – you're not going AWOL, are you?'

I laughed. 'See you in November, sir,' I said jokingly, not meaning a word of it.

9. Down but Not Out

When my leave was over, history repeated itself. I absconded from the clutches of the British Army. This time it was different as I vowed never to return, no matter what happened. The illness really took hold of me, as did the drink. I had saved some money from my time in Ireland, which I quickly pissed against the wall. Good old alcohol to numb the brain. For the first days it helped, but soon I became violent, smashing up anything in my path. There was so much pain and anger in my body, it had to find a way out. I thought I'd gone mad, I felt like a real psycho.

When someone upset me after one drinking bout, I jogged back to the squat and collected my army-issue machete. I had every intention of slicing this guy to pieces, but thankfully he was gone. For over an hour I jogged around the town, bare chested, armed with a ten-inch blade. I had murder on my mind, I wanted to kill him so much. I was no longer responsible for my actions, the normal Barry Donnan had been expelled from my body. I was a monster.

'Go and see a doctor,' my mother told me.

I did, but he could offer nothing, only tablets, but they didn't have much effect. In reality I should have been sectioned, for my own safety, and the general public's safety, but this never happened.

Week after week I struggled on, fighting almost every day, exploding at the slightest thing, lashing out at anyone. I quickly learned that drinking and PTSD don't mix. One night, after a minor incident in the local pub, a stranger approached me. 'I'll give you some advice, son. I once had a temper like yours, and I ended up killing someone. I spent ten years inside. Think about it.'

'What do you mean?'

'Calm yourself or you'll end up like me.'

'Cheers, mate.'

Inside I was deeply shocked. I realised I had become a fully-fledged psychopath quite capable of doing anything. People kept telling me how ferocious my temper was and things didn't look good. I needed help but I didn't get any. I felt as if my head were in a vice that was slowly closing, crushing my brain to oblivion. All I can remember thinking was about the futility of it all, that everything was so pointless, so useless, because we were all going to die soon. Things actually got worse, the squat was completely burnt to the ground when workmen who were tarring the roof went off for lunch and forgot about the burner. I lost all my worldly possessions, all I had were the clothes I stood in. With nowhere to go I was forced on to the streets, sleeping anywhere I could, usually in the local woods or on the beach. With no money for food I turned to a life of petty crime. I had no other choice in the matter. On the days I couldn't steal anything, I starved, but I was still alive, still here, still playing the game, worst of all I was still a serving soldier.

For 170 days I stayed on the run, until someone grassed my whereabouts to the local police, who again turned up in huge numbers. I was caught, placed in a police van and I was given a really hard time. 'You're a fucking disgrace to your regiment,' one of the cops told me. I later found out he was an ex-Royal Marine. I said nothing. 'Look at the fucking state of you.' The fucker was judging me. This was something that I had to get used to, people pointing their finger at me, making judgements, usually from the comfort of their armchair.

'Fuck off!' I said. He didn't like that and the handcuffs were tightened up.

At the police station I was dragged from the van and thrown into a cell. I cringed as the door slammed shut, it seemed to echo around the cell, drumming deep into my head. I was behind bars again. The close proximity of the cell walls made me feel vulnerable. I was trapped and alone.

'Fucking let me out!' I started screaming, at the same time kicking the door.

'Sit in there and shut up,' one of the cops warned me.

'Let me fucking go!' I shouted continually. Eventually I exploded with temper, kicking the door, screaming at the top of my voice. I completely lost control for a few minutes. After the temper passed I lay on the floor, curled up in a ball and I sobbed uncontrollably.

'Get on your feet when I come in here,' said an NCO who was from the Scots Guards, and whose job was to escort me to Edinburgh, where I'd be held until the RHF collected me. Reluctantly I stood up. 'Listen to what I'm going to say. I've got three of the biggest lads from my regiment and we're taking you to Redford Barracks, if you try anything you're for it. Do you understand?'

'Yes.'

'Yes, what?'

'Yes, Corporal.'

I was placed in handcuffs and taken through the front of the police station to an army Land Rover. The RHF wanted me back, and quickly.

'Sit there and don't fucking move,' said the NCO, shoving me in the back of the Land Rover. The three escorts glared at me. A second set of handcuffs were then used to secure me to the vehicle, this was highly illegal, but I said nothing.

The journey to Redford Barracks took over an hour and during it no one spoke a word to me. I felt like a leper, totally alone in the world. Once inside the guardroom, I was given the usual spiel by the duty policeman. 'Don't fuck me about, son. Do you hear me?'

'Yes, Corporal.'

Then I was chucked into yet another cell, alone and frightened. At that moment I could think of nothing, my mind was blank, I just couldn't carry on any more. In desperation I decided that I would escape, if and when an opportunity arose. Being caged up made me scared. Then panic set in, it was overwhelming. I just needed to get out of there, anywhere, just out.

After a couple of hours the guard commander brought me some scoff. I wasn't hungry, food was the last thing on my mind. 'I don't want it.'

'You better eat it.'

'I'm going on hunger strike.'

'You have got ten minutes, when I come back you better be finished.'

I didn't touch the food. That wasn't really the issue, the fact was that I was disobeying a direct order and therefore I was refusing to soldier. They gave me no choice. For five years the army had ruled me, not any more I decided. The discipline that had kept me going for so long had now turned into insubordination. They could all fuck off. Sure enough, the guard commander returned. He wasn't very happy. 'You're for the fucking high-jump, you wanker,' he was shouting.

'Kiss my arse,' I said, shocking myself. For the first time in my life I was fighting back.

'Do you know who you are speaking to?'

'I don't give a toss.'

He then squared up to me. I was being threatened. He said he was going to kill me.

'Go for it,' I said with complete disrespect.

For a few seconds we stared at each other, then he turned and walked from the cell. My mind was in turmoil. I started doing press-ups and other exercises, anything to keep the mind occupied. The enemy were trying to break me but I couldn't give in. Every few minutes the enemy started checking up on me, looking through the hatch in the cell door, sussing me out. I ignored them, I continued on my exercise routine. I don't know how long I was in the holding cell, it couldn't have been more than six hours, but it seemed like a lifetime. At some point an escort from the RHF arrived, four blokes in total, two from my old platoon, but I was in such a state I didn't recognise them. For me they were the enemy and I was the outsider. I had finally cracked up and become a total mental case.

'We're taking you back to Oakington,' the escort commander told me.

'Where?'

'Oakington.'

Time was slipping back and forward. Where was I? How did I get here? Nothing made any sense. Was this another dream, or was it for real? Why was everyone shouting at me? In my mind nothing was in order. Did the Gulf War finish yesterday or was that Lockerbie? They were all talking about me, but I couldn't hear a word, even though I was standing beside them.

From Redford I was taken back to Cambridge in a hired car, and again I was handcuffed to the door to make sure I had no chance of escape. We reached Oakington in the early hours of the morning to find the duty cop had waited up especially for me. Inside the guardroom I was told to strip naked, my civilian clothes were taken from me and in exchange I was given a pair of army overalls.

'What's happening to my clothes?'

'They will be destroyed.'

'You can't do that,' I protested.

'I can do what I want.'

It certainly looked that way. I never saw the clothing again.

'Follow me,' I was ordered.

For the millionth time I was turfed into a cold, damp cell, alone. I was now a prisoner-of-war. An hour or so later, I was ordered through to the front. I checked the clock on the wall, it was 0425 hours in the bloody morning.

'Get a brush and start cleaning up.'

'Yes, Corporal.'

For the next three hours I cleaned the inside of the guard-room. I was an expert, the place was gleaming. The powers that be were just fucking me about, giving me a hard time for the sake of it. Unknown to them I was treading a very fine line. I was very unwell. First thing after breakfast, which I refused to eat, I was marched in front of the CO and, after a bollocking, I was told to get a grip and pull myself together.

'You will be held in close arrest until such times as a court-martial can be arranged. Now get out of my sight,' the CO shouted. That was the first time I'd ever heard him raise his voice. 'March out, Donnan.'

Back at the guardroom there were problems: the regiment was flying to Belize in a week's time so I would have to be transferred elsewhere until my court-martial. Within an hour a suitable holding cell was found. I was moved to the Queen's Division Depot in Bassingbourne. It was not good news as I would be cut off completely from the RHF. They were deserting me. It seemed as if no one wanted me in their guard-room. All the moving about was not helping me very much. As the hours ticked past I went deeper into the system. At 1000 hours I was taken under escort on the short trip across to Bassingbourne, which was a training depot. After some paper-work was completed, I was shown to my new cell. It was tiny and I didn't even have a bed, just a poxy mattress on the floor.

It felt strange in my new surroundings and the smell of the place made me feel sick. I started unpacking my kit, with tears streaming down my face. I had nowhere to turn. 'Doonan!' came the shout.

I doubled to the front desk and halted.

'My name is Corporal Welsh, when I shout you run through here and put your toes on the brass line,' he said in a strong cockney accent.

'Yes, Corporal.'

'As you are aware this is a training depot and you will not be treated any differently from the recruits?'

'But, Corporal . . .' I started protesting.

'Listen to me, I don't give a fuck how long you've been in the army, this is my guardroom and you'll abide by my rules.'

'Yes, Corporal,' I lied.

'Oh, and get the kettle on, milk and two for me.'

As I boiled the kettle I realised they were going to give me a really hard time. Look at it from their side, I was a Scottish soldier stuck inside an English training depot, awaiting a second court-martial, in other words I was scum. For the next two hours I was treated accordingly, making tea, polishing the floor, running around like a fucking madman.

'Doonan!'

'Corporal,' I replied, as I doubled through and stood on the brass line.

'Outside for lunch,' ordered Corporal Welsh.

'My name is Donnan,' I told him.

'Just get outside.'

I walked outside and stood at attention.

'Go to the pace I call out, Doonan, by the front, quick march!' The pace was in double-quick time, no one could have marched that fast. He was fucking me about. 'Mark time!'

I stopped marching forward and marked time on the spot. I was really struggling.

'Get your fucking knees up,' said the cockney bastard.

At that moment a recruit platoon was marching past, blokes who'd been in the army only a few weeks. That was all the encouragement he needed, he was showing me off, making an example of me, proving to the recruits that this was what happened if you were a bad boy.

'Get yourself moving – or you'll be getting no lunch,' he was screaming now, right in my ear. The cockney accent was drilling into my brain, irritating me greatly. I was working hard to keep the pace going, I could go no faster. 'We can stay here all day if you want, you wanker!' At that point I stopped marching and stood still. I'd had it. 'What the fuck do you think you're doing?' The worm turned.

I exploded, rage consumed me. Without thinking I smashed him in the face and he dropped to the ground unconscious. I turned around and walked the short distance to the guardroom. Casually, I walked past the provost sergeant and through the back into my cell, leaving the door wide open. What happened next or in what order it happened I'm not sure, but I started smashing up the cell. I had lost it. All the years of bottling things up, all the hurt and anger, were now showing. One or two of the hierarchy, including the RSM and the adjutant, appeared at the cell door. 'If anybody comes in here, I'll fucking kill him!' I screamed. No one dared even shut my cell door. They were frightened, but so was I. Time passed. I lay sobbing on the ground, my hands were sore with punching the walls. At one point I even turned on myself, punching into my face and pulling my own hair.

Next thing I remember is the medical officer appearing beside me. He was there for a good while before he said anything. 'This soldier is unfit for detention, get him out of here and across to the medical centre now,' ordered the doctor, who was also a full colonel.

'He isn't one of ours, sir,' added the provost sergeant.

'I don't care,' said the colonel abruptly.

the cell I was walked over to the medical centre where heavily sedated. The drugs started taking effect within nutes. 'Don't worry, everything is okay, we'll look after you,' said the doctor, comforting me. It had taken someone from another regiment to help me. The fact that the doctor was a colonel and he held the position of commander medical for the whole brigade certainly helped. 'Jail is the last place you should be,' he told me.

I was shown upstairs to a bed and told to lie down, soon I was drowsy and fell asleep. For two days I stayed in bed. I was heavily drugged and could do nothing. While I was out of it, the doctor had phoned the RHF and demanded my medical notes. He was furious. He diagnosed severe post-traumatic stress disorder, which the RHF already knew about, they had just brushed it aside continually. Once my notes arrived, the colonel went nuts as everything was there in black and white: Lockerbie, Belize, the Gulf War, my long periods of absence and, of course, my stints in the jail. Basically, the army had known about my PTSD for nearly 18 months, yet they still court-martialled me and sent me to Northern Ireland and, worse still, they were preparing for a second court-martial. The doctor told me I should sue them for negligence. I promised him I would. Colonel Blackwell was my guardian angel, he saved my life, without him God knows what would have happened.

'I'm sending you to the psychiatric ward in Woolwich where they will be able to look after you better. I don't have the facilities here,' he said.

'Yes, sir.'

'If you have any problems, phone me.'

'Thank you, sir,' I slurred, not fully aware of my surroundings.

From Bassingbourne I was transported to the Queen Elizabeth Military Hospital in south London. I thought that at last someone was going to help me, but the times of injustice were not over just yet.

Ward five in Woolwich is where the army d
psychiatric problems. It wasn't full of loonies as I expe
half a dozen or so fucked-up soldiers, blokes who had
too much. For the first time in years I felt quite safe, maybe it
was the drugs they were pumping me full of. After a quick
medical I was given a bed and I lay down.

Much of what happened over the next few days I can't
remember clearly, it is locked away deep in my mind, so deeply
I can't access it, maybe that's a good thing, I don't know. Yet
some bits I can recall with amazing clarity, like when they told
me I wouldn't have to face another court-martial and that I
suffered from PTSD.

Nothing very constructive was done, it just seemed tablets
were the answer, but I wasn't complaining as for a week or so
they calmed me down. Attempts to engage me in
psychotherapy were useless as I now resented everyone in
uniform. I was hostile and I found the doctors liked
pontificating, talking shit, claiming to be experts in PTSD. I
realised there were no medical experts in this field. We are the
experts, the people who suffer it, anyone else can't even imagine
how it feels.

Drugs, drugs and more drugs, that was the cure.

One night a new psychiatrist sat and listened while four of us
talked about our experiences, and for nearly two hours the
quack listened in. What happened afterwards is a good example
of them not understanding. The quack was so traumatised by
what he heard that he was off work for a week and had to have
some counselling.

Many of the blokes had horror stories to tell, and mine was
in no way unique. We were all fucked up in the head, mentally
unwell. We all stuck together, as if we were in some exclusive
club.

At night-time the ward was an eerie place. Some blokes
wandered around like zombies, while others were screaming

and shouting in their sleep. Most nights I would wake up in a cold, feverish sweat, not knowing what the nightmares were about, I was frightened though. Slipping back into sleep for a while, then it would happen again. Sometimes the dreams seemed so lifelike, so vivid. It became difficult to separate real life and what was a dream, everything merged into one. My body was numb, but that suited me.

At some stage a newcomer appeared on the ward. I don't remember much about him due to the drugs but what I do know is that at first he was very quiet, but then he changed. He was a young guy and hadn't been in the army very long but that didn't stop him from being really mouthy. During a therapy session on the afternoon of his arrival, we had big fucking problems, the gobshite stood up and verbally attacked a few of the blokes. 'You lot don't want to get better,' he said. I could hardly believe this cunt. Two minutes in the place and he was already mouthing off. One thing about people with PTSD, they never judge anyone.

'I'll fucking kill you!' I shouted, not meaning it literally.

Anyway, this clown upset everyone on the ward, most of us had a hard enough time with the army, never mind fellow patients, making comments. Gobshite was moved to another wing of the hospital for his own safety. The medical staff really believed I would kill him, or so they said. Thinking about it now, I wish I had.

The next scene in this story of my downfall was that another patient and I sneaked over the fence and escaped into the town of Woolwich. We had one thing in mind, to get pissed.

'Two lagers, mate, please,' I said to the barman.

We must have looked a fine pair. My buddy was a paranoid schizophrenic and I wasn't very far behind him. After two hours we were totally spaced out. Drinking and medication don't go together very well, certainly not then, anyway. Both of us were so edgy we watched the door continually, never turning our backs for a second. At closing time we staggered back to the military hospital out of our tiny minds. Ward five was very busy, I can remember that, usually it was a skeleton staff at night, but everyone was still working and hanging around. I thought it strange.

Gobshite had caused a huge tidal wave of emotion amongst the patients and tensions were running very high indeed.

'Barry, come here and talk to me,' said one of the doctors. I grabbed a chair and sat opposite him. 'May I remind you that you're still a serving soldier and are under Queen's regulations?'

'I don't fucking need you to tell me that, I've experienced Queen's regs first hand,' I said bluntly.

'Have you been drinking?' he asked.

'I've had a couple.'

'How do you feel about what happened today?'

'Here we go,' I thought, 'psycho-babble bullshit, a bit fucking late to start talking about things now.' I got up and walked away.

'Barry, come back!' he was shouting.

'Fuck off!'

I walked towards my bed, anger ripped through me, then I lost control. In a fit of temper I headbutted a large pane of glass, which instantly smashed. As soon as it happened I knew it was big mistake, so I ran and hid in the next ward, which was empty. After a short time several of my fellow patients joined me and we stayed there for a couple of hours. Eventually, tiredness took over and we all headed back to the ward together, where there was a big surprise in store for us. The medical staff had called in an armed guard and the Royal Military Police, who also sent in a nice big Alsatian as a deterrent. It was immediately a them-and-us scenario, which quickly got out of hand. Several of us were attacked and grabbed, and at one point they threatened to set the hound on us.

'I'll bite its fucking ears off,' I shouted to the dog-handler. That stopped them in their tracks. But by then it was too late, the officer in charge ordered us to the jail. Even though two weeks before I had been released as unfit to be in detention, they still went ahead and slammed me up.

I was thrown in a cell belonging to the Royal Artillery Training Regiment, which was more or less opposite the hospital, handy or what? Once again I was heavily drugged so I don't remember very much about it. The following day I was booted out of hospital and sent back to face another court-martial. My regiment was in Belize, so they put me in the guardroom of 39 Engineer Regiment where I stayed for over a week. During this time, the Grim Reaper came to visit me, he tapped me on the shoulder and told me it was time to go. I swallowed a concoction of tablets and waited for death. Nothing happened. The tablets must have been Smarties or something, but I was still alive. The next day I was transferred to Colchester and they put me into the block with some serious prisoners: squaddies who had committed murder. For three weeks the army kept me in solitary confinement, until my local MP intervened.

I was never allowed back to the military hospital as they said I was aggressive and dangerous, but wasn't it the army who made me that way? My second court-martial was scrapped and they booted me out of the army on medical grounds: the diagnosis was severe post-traumatic stress disorder. The army dumped me in civvy street, my illness still untreated. Nothing had changed, the only difference was that I was out of the army. The battle was just beginning.

10. Legalities

In February 1995, nearly three years after my discharge, I decided I wanted justice from the army. My lawyer advised me that I had a very strong case against the British Army on several different grounds. Our first task was to get an independent psychiatrist to examine me. His report confirmed I had PTSD, also that it was 'highly likely' I was suffering at the time of the first court-martial. We then contacted the MoD. It took them almost nine months to write back, not bad going.

Our next task was to obtain legal aid to raise an action for damages in the court of session against the MoD. It was refused on grounds of a time bar. They said I was outside my three-year period, so we lodged an appeal. Again it was refused. This time they said it was for a different reason than the first instance, but they didn't tell me what it was. We appealed again, they refused again, this time giving a new set of reasons. All in all this happened six times. It was never going to get near the court.

My local MP even lobbied the Armed Forces Minister at that time, but it was fruitless. In March 1997 my case hit the national press and TV, but still the MoD ignored me. The battle also took its toll on my health, several times I nearly gave in, but I know that's what they wanted. I kept fighting on, but to no avail.

Then I heard about the European Court of Human Rights. I

applied with the details of my case, which they accepted. A decision is expected this year at some time, and justice may be finally done. It will be a test case against the army and it could quite easily open the floodgates for other veterans. I certainly hope so. The MoD have managed to ignore us for many years, but time is running out. My case has taken a couple of very strange twists and turns. For security reasons I can't say at the moment, but I can assure you it's shocking stuff.

I will fight all my life against the army, against those who robbed me of my future and a decent past. Nothing can ever compensate me for all the years of mental anguish. I just want the army to admit they made a few mistakes, but I feel that will never happen. Gulf War syndrome has also started to rear its ugly head, but that's another story. For me, the whole thing has been a long, lonely battle.

If the MoD could give me a new brain, one free of all the memories and nightmares, then I'd be happy. But that's just being stupid. The day justice is done is the day I will start living again.